Becky

Becky

Bits and Pieces of the Life of Becky Meyers as
told by her Mother, Holly von Helms

HOLLY VON HELMS

ISBN-13: 9781530687541
ISBN-10: 1530687543

BECKY

(Bits and Pieces of the Life of Becky Meyers)
as told by her Mother, Holly von Helms

Flashback

The hot flash woke me from a deep sleep, its heat scorching my inner core and slowly moving outward. It covered me like scalding rain. Sitting bolt upright in bed, suddenly, and for no special reason, my thoughts went back to Becky's delivery. In the middle of the night, flapping the covers to cool off, miserable from this most unwelcome aspect of middle age, I relived every moment of her birth and became enraged. It was 1990, for crying out loud. Becky was now a 29-year-old woman. "Why now?" I asked myself. "Where did this rage come from?"

The hot flash subsided; my body heat receded back to normal, and I couldn't go back to sleep. The memories of her delivery kept flashing through my thoughts like lightning after the thunderclap. The pictures of that fated day flooded my brain and sleep was not to come again that night.

It was September 4, 1961, Labor Day, believe it or not, when I went into labor with Becky. She was due August 28th, but decided to come on Labor Day. That day my mother and I traipsed out to Cheyenne Canyon in Colorado Springs to watch the Fort Carson Mountaineers do their maneuvers on the cliffs. I huffed and puffed and with great effort lifted each foot to meet each oncoming step up the steep trail to the observation point. It was a hard climb and many people were coming down. When we reached the top, we were informed that the event had been cancelled. Wouldn't you think one of those folks descending would have looked at this very pregnant woman and said, "Don't keep climbing, honey, it's been cancelled." Not one person paid the least bit of attention to my condition.

That night, a little before midnight, I was aroused by cramping in my abdomen. I thought I was having gas pains and finally went into my Mother's bedroom and complained about the fact that I couldn't relieve the pressure. She bounded out of bed and calmly suggested that we call the doctor. (We were living with her that summer in Colorado Springs between my husband Don's graduation and graduate school, and this was my first pregnancy.) I expected, from all the horror stories I had heard about delivery, that my water would break first. Who ever heard of phantom gas pains being the first indication of labor starting? Not I.

The Birth

My doctor happened to be out of town. Against my wishes and better judgment, I had to be delivered by his associate, Dr. Kerr, at a hospital not of my choice. I had worked at the Colorado Springs Medical Center where they practiced, and Dr. Kerr was the least compassionate doctor I had ever observed in my life. Pregnant patients were herded through his office like so many cattle being loaded on a truck. He was cold and distant and unfeeling, and I had no other choice.

Don, and I jumped in our little 1948 Chevy coupe and headed for the hospital. Not one block from Mother's house, we ran out of gas. What is the Boy Scout Motto? Oh, yes, 'Be Prepared'. The father of my yet unborn child had never been a Boy Scout, not that it would have made a difference. He, the track star, sprinted back to the house and borrowed one of my stepfather's three cars, which is another story for the telling. We arrived at the hospital in due time, no pun intended, and I checked in.

A large, pasty-faced nurse prepped me; the doctor examined me, and then ordered 200 ccs of something with a whisper in the nurse's ear. I heard the '200 ccs' and asked, "Is that a pain killer? "

He snarled, "Yes, it is," with impatience dripping from his words.

I informed him that I did not want a painkiller, and that I would request one when and if I felt I needed one. I had already agreed to a spinal block based on the advice of my doctor. In hindsight, he advised on false bases, but in those days doctors were not contradicted or their wisdom doubted. I had been a swimming instructor. In fact, I had taught his daughter to swim. He convinced me that with all my swimming, the "thick" muscles I had developed in the pelvic area would make a delivery very difficult and painful. In addition he convinced me that it would be much better for the baby. Was I going to argue with that? I took his word for it.

I never asked for the painkiller, but one was administered some time during those interminable morning hours. I was in too much pain to protest. A little before nine o'clock I was wheeled into the delivery room.

Just an aside: it was the day after Labor Day, a Tuesday to be exact. If you've ever tried to get a doctor's appointment on the day after a long weekend, you know that the line is busy for minutes on end or you are put on hold for what seems like hours. Dr. Kerr, being the only one in the office that day, was in one big hurry to get to where the money was, his office and his waiting patients, and I was not one of his regular patients.

(Now, back to the delivery room.)

Labor was going as it should; the pains were getting stronger, but I had not yet reached the pushing stage. I can say this in retrospect, having had two other children since Becky and learning through those deliveries what the sequence of events includes. I had no idea what to expect with my first baby. In his haste to get my delivery over with, Dr. Kerr injected the anesthetic for the spinal, but it was too early in the labor process. Paralyzed by the medication, my muscles quit working, and there was my baby, stuck in the birth canal.

I could hear the doctor and the nurse muttering under the sheet, which covered my lower extremities like an improvised tent. I finally asked, "Where is my baby?"

The response was, "We're working on the head."

An eon seemed to pass, and again I asked, "Where is my baby?"

"We're still working on the head," he responded with some frustration in his voice.

They continued to mutter and struggle and again I asked, "Where is my baby?"

The response this time was, "We're working on the shoulders."

The next response to my repetitive question was, "We're working on the buttocks."

Even though I knew nothing about delivering a baby, I knew something wasn't right with this scenario.

An indeterminable length of time had passed since they wheeled me into the delivery room. I had no idea how much time really passed, but I was beside myself. Why wasn't my baby out of my belly yet? Why was it taking so long and why were the doctor and nurse so secretive? Somewhere in my woman's intuition I knew this was not the normal procedure.

Finally they pulled out her little body with the announcement, "It's a girl!" She was held by her feet, hanging upside down, and smacked on the buttocks. Nothing. He smacked her again, and again no sound came from her tiny mouth. With the fifth slap on the rear end she let out a cry. My heart was thumping like a giant drum and the relief was overwhelming. Letting out an enormous sigh, I thought to myself, "My baby is all right". Little did I know. They whisked her away, and I didn't see her for the next twenty-four hours.

Blood in my colostrum was the reason given for my not being able to hold my baby, and I was also informed that nursing was out of the question until they determined the source of the blood. Twenty-four hours later they brought her to me, the most precious bundle I had ever held. She had dark curly hair and a rather large nose. The nurse informed me that the bruises on her cheeks were due to the forceps delivery. In addition, the sutures on the top of her head were overlapping for the same reason. I learned that from the pediatrician at a later date. It was felt that condition alone might impede the normal development of her brain.

My dearest and oldest friend in the world is a Jewish woman, Marilyn Ganetsky. Chuckling, she entered the hospital room and informed me that because of Becky's dark hair and her big 'schnoz', the bruises giving the appearance of dark skin, and with a name like Rebecca Meyers everyone thought she was a Jewish baby. We both laughed long and hard.

I was able to feed Becky a bottle, which she took ravenously, and for the next four days she was brought to me at feeding time. My pediatrician visited her in the nursery and informed me that she had a very traumatic delivery and would probably be a very nervous, tense baby. I paid very little attention to that information in my joy at holding my firstborn.

On the fifth day we were released from the hospital and handed the bill. I noticed that there was a charge for an oxygen tent. Inquiring about the reason for the charge, it was related to me that the doctor didn't like her color, so he gave her oxygen for four days. Nothing had been said to us about any problem with her delivery. It was all very "behind the scenes." Oh, that the APGAR test had been in existence in those days and the mask for applying oxygen as the head emerges from the birth canal.

We took our precious newborn home and thus began our journey. She was a very complacent, quiet and cooperative newborn. I fed her when it was time for her to be hungry, not because she was fussy. We were so lucky to have such a good baby, we thought.

At her first examination at the age of two weeks, the pediatrician noticed that it was difficult to turn her head to the right to examine her left ear. Upon closer examination he diagnosed congenital torticollis, a tightening of the cervical muscles. It was a result of the difficult forceps delivery she had endured. Apparently the neck muscles had been stretched during the procedure, and in healing had contracted pulling her head to the left. The prescription was to hold her shoulder stable and turn her head in the opposite direction several times a day for six weeks. Thank God he gave us such good advice, because her head does not hang to one side, as it would have had he not discovered that subtle birth injury.

The First Year

We returned to Boulder so her father could continue his education as a graduate student at the University of Colorado, and for the first three months she seemed to develop normally. She remained a very happy, placid baby. She rolled over and off the bed one day. I had no idea she was capable of turning over. I was mortified. Bless Dr. Spock. His book became my Bible.

When referring to the chapter on childhood accidents, he assured me that any mother who watched her child so closely that such things couldn't happen, was an overprotective mother. It assuaged my guilt, but I never left her unattended on any surface higher than the floor after that.

She didn't seem able to track an object when it was passed in front of her eyes. That concerned me until her grandfather came to visit. He passed his bright, shiny cigarette lighter in front of her eyes and she followed it wherever he moved. It was such a relief and reassured me she was just fine. He told me not to worry, and I took his word for it, for the time being. I tried to put concern about her development out of my mind and just enjoyed her for the good baby that she was.

Becky at 6 months

She sat up at seven months, well within the normal range, but crawling was much delayed. The small motel unit where we lived had a floor register that was about 2 feet square. After she burned her hand once, I decided she would not be allowed on the floor again. She spent her waking hours sitting in a wheeled walker. With hard-soled shoes on her little feet, she was able to maneuver around the tiny living room safely. Not only did the walker delay her crawling, in my estimation it also affected her ability to learn to walk.

During this same period of development I noticed when she reached for a cracker or another object, she didn't use a pincher grasp. She rotated her wrist outward, grasped the cracker in the valley between the thumb and forefinger, then turned her hand back toward her face so she could put it in her mouth. It was a very awkward movement but worked for her.

As her development continued to slow down, I tried to avoid comparing her to other children her age. It was very obvious that something was awry. I began asking the pediatrician during our monthly visits, "Why isn't she doing things like other babies her age?"

His reply was always, "Don't worry, Mother, she'll be fine."

She crawled at ten months. We had moved to my mother's home in Colorado Springs for the summer where she was able to have free range of the entire house. Crawling at ten months was still within the 'normal' range for average babies, though very near the end of that range. Again, I chose not to dwell on her apparent developmental delays, hoping against hope that she was a 'normal', healthy baby.

The next step on the developmental charts was walking. When she was a year old, I began questioning the doctor about her inability or unwillingness to walk. She could pull herself up on the furniture she could reach and ambulate around it, but at fifteen months she was still not taking unsupported steps. The doctor assured me that the average age for walking was fifteen months, so I **had** to know that many babies started walking well beyond that age. Again, he consoled me and told me not to worry, reassuring me that she would be fine. I wanted so much to believe him.

"I think she's retarded."

The next year we moved into the army barracks on Water Street in Boulder. Her father was in his second year of graduate school and I was pregnant with our second child. I babysat two little sisters to augment our income, and life was good. Becky was not keeping up with her peers, but I had decided to just let things be as they would be. She was happy and healthy, and that's all that mattered to me.

When she was eighteen months old she woke up in the middle of the night. She was burning up with fever and had no muscle control. She was like a rag doll, and her pupils were completely unfocused. I was scared silly. I called the doctor and reached his on-call physician who told me to give her an alcohol rub and a baby aspirin. He told me she would be fine in the morning. I hung up the phone and sat down and cried. Who knew how to give a baby an alcohol rub? Not me. I'd never heard of such a thing.

Becky age 1

8

Dousing a washcloth with rubbing alcohol, I dabbed it on her forehead, gave her a baby aspirin, and put her in bed with me. Her father was competing with the United States track team in Japan, and I was home alone with Becky and her baby sister, Cindy, who was two months old at the time. I felt alone and helpless and finally dropped off to sleep with Becky in my arms. She slept peacefully through the night, but the next morning awoke with the same symptoms. Taken off guard by this turn of events and really frightened by her condition, I called the doctor and this time was relieved to reach our pediatrician. He suggested I bring her in to see him as soon as possible. I contacted a neighbor who agreed to watch Cindy and left for his office. The pediatrician, Dr. Takahashi, examined her thoroughly, listened to my description of her symptoms and reactions, and, looking into my eyes, said in a very matter-of-fact manner, " I think it's encephalitis."

I took a deep breath and, swallowing my tears, asked with trepidation, "That's sleeping sickness, isn't it?"

He answered by saying, "That's one form of it, yes. Children die from it. I want to put her in the hospital, see how she responds to treatment, and, if she pulls through this, I want you to have her evaluated, because I think she is mentally retarded." Just like that.

Boom!!! It felt like he had taken a double-barreled shotgun, pulled the trigger and hit me in the gut. She was to be hospitalized and observed and only time would tell. I took her to the hospital where they put her in a small hospital gown and handed me her empty pajamas. They took her temperature and immediately began filling a large tub with water, added buckets of ice, and immersed my darling child into it with no compunction to do it slowly and mercifully. She screamed and reached for me, but I was helpless. They would not let me near her. I thought the bottom had fallen out of my life. Sobbing, I left to make arrangements for my mother to come and help with Cindy, Becky's empty pajamas in hand as a reminder of what could happen. All the way home the thought of never being able to put them on her again haunted me.

When I got back to the barracks, my neighbor's husband had managed, after several strategic phone calls, to reach Becky's dad in Hawaii on a layover from Japan. He soon called, and when I told him about the possibility of mental retardation, he said, "All we can do is love her and accept her for who she is." Blessed words coming from his mouth.

My mother, who was still working after all these years, dropped everything and sped to Boulder from Colorado Springs. She went with me to the hospital to see how Becky was faring. Becky's favorite thing in the whole wide world at that point in her life was to go through my purse. When we entered the room she was standing up supporting herself on the railing. She saw her grandma and me and reached for mother's purse and said, "Poose?" With that simple gesture, we knew she was going to be all right. Tears of relief ran down our cheeks as we laughed with glee, knowing she would survive.

Once the fever had subsided she responded normally. The diagnosis turned out to be German measles that refused to erupt. The lack of muscle and eye control was a reaction to the high fever, a form of seizure activity. We took her home three days later, righter than rain, except for the sinister specter of mental retardation hanging over our heads.

A Few Steps

Every day at lunchtime, with Cindy napping, Becky and I would wait in the front yard for her father to come home for lunch. I would stand her up, walk a few paces from her and then hold out my arms, encouraging her to walk to me. She would take three steps and sit down. Day after day, time after time we would try to walk. One day a well meaning neighbor walked by and said, "She's never gonna walk. Why don't you just quit trying?" But we just kept practicing. I envisioned the day when she would run and jump into her father's arms as he came down the walk.

Becky age 20 months

In reality, I felt like I had twins. Cindy and Becky were 16 months apart and almost at the same level of development by the time Becky's second summer had passed. We had moved to Colorado Springs in June because they were tearing down the barracks, and we had no place to live in Boulder. My mother was gracious enough to let us stay with her while my husband completed his graduate school requirements. We all tried to help Becky walk, but walk she would not. She was a most efficient crawler.

She had a constitution like an elephant. I taught swimming that summer and hired a young woman to watch the kids. The sitter called me at the pool to inform me that Becky had swallowed a stone. I told her not to worry. Kids eat dirt and don't die, so I assured her that all would be fine. I pictured a small pebble, rounded and smooth, that would go down easily and not be a problem in passing through her digestive tract. The sitter was relieved that I wasn't upset.

The next morning Becky's diaper held a much bigger surprise than the stone in my mind's eye. The stone was rounded and smooth, and about an inch in diameter. She passed it with no trouble at all, a symbol of the fortitude and constitution it was going to take to get her through life as it came at her in torrents. She had more ups and downs coming her way than any of us could have imagined.

Back to Boulder

In September, we moved back to Boulder to teach school and finish Don's Master's degree. We found a two-bedroom apartment at the corner of Portland Place and Ninth Street. It consisted of two ell-shaped buildings with apartments on two levels. We were fortunate to have rented a ground level apartment. Don was off somewhere, and the girls and I were trying to get settled into our new home. Cindy was taking a nap and Becky was crawling and underfoot. I was afraid I was either going to step on her or trip over her.

Since she could only crawl, I felt safe putting her right outside the front door by a mud puddle with several toys to keep her busy. I figured that I could keep an eye on her and she couldn't crawl very far before I could catch her. I puttered about for about ten minutes and went to check on her. She was gone! I mean she was not within fifty feet of the front door. Trying to keep myself calm, I dropped everything and headed out the door. As I looked about the large yard, I noticed a small playground area at the southwest corner of the lot. A wire fence enclosed a merry-go-round, swings and a slide, and there, thankfully, was Becky _walking_ from one apparatus to the next. I nearly fainted from relief and was overwhelmed with disbelief. She just decided it would be easier to walk that distance than to crawl, so she got up on her feet and walked. She was two years old. She never crawled again. She still walks with a forward head and rounded shoulders just like she did that first day.

Trials and Tribulations

After Dr. Takahashi suggested Becky might be 'retarded,' we started the process of having her evaluated. Children's Hospital of Denver was recommended to us, and we made an appointment for June 1964. That was more than a year away, and the wait was only made easier by the fact that I was teaching part time and raising two little girls. I really didn't have a lot of time to think about the outcome of the testing.

As each month passed, it became more obvious that Becky was definitely delayed in her development. She and Cindy started walking at the same time. Cindy was nine months old; Becky was a little over two years old. They both gave up the bottle in the same month, Cindy at eleven months, Becky at twenty-eight months. I decided then that I would turn Becky loose and encourage her to keep up with her baby sister, rather than trying to hold Cindy back. Cindy was the best thing that ever happened to Becky. Becky followed her everywhere, and anything Cindy could do, Becky was willing to try. She ambled up the stairs at the apartment building one day and proceeded to tumble down two or three steps to the ground. I comforted her and turned her loose again. Her father was aghast. Was I really going to let her do that again? My response to him was "I can't protect her from stairs all her life, now can I? She needs to learn how to walk up and down stairs correctly."

I decided that Becky would stay with us regardless of the results of her evaluation. I had been told horror stories of post-evaluation suggestions and recommendations, one of which was institutionalization. All my arguments were in my head and ready to use at a moment's notice. The coming evaluation process and the hope that Becky would come through with shining colors consumed my thoughts. It was a pipe dream, but it sustained me.

In April 1964, when Cindy was but 15 months old, she came home from her well-baby checkup at the county health department, and grimaced every time she tried to look up at me. It was as if it hurt to extend her neck. That night, with her father in Denver at a meeting, she developed a fever of 104.6 degrees. I called the doctor and again reached an on call pediatrician, Dr. Gillette. His wife told me that he was at the hospital in a meeting. She would have him call me as soon as she could reach him.

He did call and suggested that I give Cindy some weak tea and wait to see if she could keep it down. As I held her, she felt as if she were burning up. I took her temperature again, and it had risen to 106. I called Dr. Gillette's wife and told her to have the doctor meet me in the emergency room. In haste, I left Becky with a neighbor and hurried to the hospital. A nurse met me at the door, put Cindy in a big metal crib and said to me with disdain, "Doesn't feel like 106 to me!" I invited her to be my guest and take Cindy's temperature herself.

"My God, it's 106.2," she exclaimed. At which moment Cindy proceeded to have a grand mal seizure. It was such a relief to have that occur while she was in the emergency room. I might have panicked at home had that happened there.

Dr. Gillette examined Cindy forthwith and decided to do a spinal tap. The test results showed pneumococcal meningitis. He assured me that, with antibiotic treatment, she would be a different baby the next morning. They stabilized her legs with sandbags and inserted an IV into her little thigh. I left her there with great reluctance. I had to go home and retrieve Becky from the neighbor's and wait for her father to come home so I could inform him of her hospitalization.

I knew she was in good hands, and what could I do besides just fret?

When I arrived at the hospital early the next morning, Dr. Takahashi, our regular pediatrician, was there. I asked him if he were there to see Cindy. He didn't even know she had been admitted. He looked at her chart, examined her and said, "There is no doubt about the meningitis. I think we can pull her through." This is the same doctor who implied that if Becky lived through encephalitis, he wanted her tested for mental retardation. I decided in that instant that he would no longer be our pediatrician. I needed someone with a gentler, more empathetic bedside manner. I had a hard row to hoe ahead of me. I didn't need such blatant disregard for a mother's feelings and sensitivities.

As it turned out, Cindy also had influenza in her meninges, a bug that would have killed her ten years prior. Once that was discovered and treated, she perked up, and, to the amazement of the doctor, had no residual hearing or vision loss, which often accompany meningitis. It was not an easy time for us, but it did take our minds off Becky and her forthcoming evaluation.

Evaluation

On June 2, 1964 we traipsed down to Denver for our intake interview with the evaluation team at Children's Hospital. We answered all their questions and were informed that we should be there with Becky on July 20th, that same summer.

Becky was almost three years old, knew right from wrong and required little, if any, discipline. She was easy going, always happy, though not potty trained. She was a delightful child. Sometimes I would forget that she allegedly had so many problems. She seemed almost "normal" to me in spite of her limitations.

When we arrived at the hospital in July, she was taken away from us, crying and reaching back with her arms outstretched. It was with utter disbelief that we realized that she had to go through hours of testing all by herself in a strange place with strange people. We assumed that we would be able to accompany her through the many steps of the evaluation. Sitting in the waiting room we could hear her sobbing down the

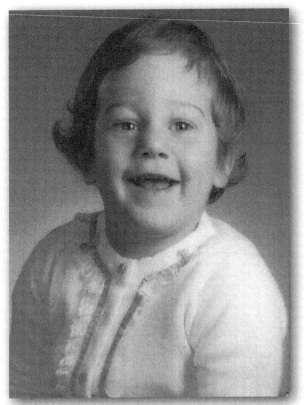

Becky age 3

hall. I begged to be taken away from there. Listening to her cry was more than I could stand.

We wandered down to Larimer Street, now known as LoDo, which at that time was known for the ne'er-do-wells and homeless alcoholics who slept in the gutters. We walked among the hapless residents to a pawnshop where we purchased my first guitar for about $40. It was an early birthday present and meant to keep my mind off what was happening to my child at the hospital.

We arrived back at the testing center before Becky was finished with the psychologist. We could tell he was disgruntled and unhappy with her performance. His implications were that she was uncooperative and spoiled. What did he know? She was so happy to see us; she fell into my arms and sobbed. Did I feel guilty? You bet I did. This was only the first day of testing. We had to go through this for two more days.

She was given a test to determine her IQ and behavior patterns, given an EEG to determine seizure activity, put through a complete physical examination including blood tests, and a myriad of other tests. She was kept busy for two full days of testing and was literally a basket case at the end of the evaluation. Not only were they trying to determine a baseline for her intelligence, but also they were looking for causative factors and diagnoses.

Genetics

I had an uncle with Down syndrome. He was my mother's brother and born when my grandmother was forty-five years old. Uncle Harry was with us our whole lives. My grandmother put him in a home when he flunked kindergarten for the second time. In the 1940's that was common practice. He later was placed in the state institution in Wheatridge for 35 years; lived at home with my Grandmother for several years; was placed in a residential living situation; and ultimately moved into the same nursing home to which his mother had been admitted.

Because Harry was part of our family, the hospital decided it wanted Becky to have a chromosomal evaluation. The appointment was made at Colorado University's Medical School and was scheduled for sometime in October 1964. They wanted to rule out genetic causes before they determined the source of Becky's delays.

I bundled both girls up that October and drove from Fort Collins to Denver. Don had been hired as the track coach at Colorado State University in 1964. The Medical School was south and east of the downtown area. Parking was not an easy thing to find even then. Struggling with a 21 month old and a three year old, I worked my way from the car to the reception area. Becky was admitted and we were directed to the testing area. Again, they took her from me and forbade me to go with her.

They put her in a room and shut the door. Cindy and I found a place to sit and looked at children's books and watched people passing by.

It seemed like hours had passed, and I picked up Cindy and meandered down the hall to check on the progress of the testing. I opened the door of the examining room just in time to see three adults holding Becky down while the doctor came at her with a syringe, big enough for an elephant, aimed at her carotid artery. I hugged Cindy close to my body, and turned and ran down the hall as fast as I could go. I couldn't believe what they were doing to my child and I just had to escape. Again I felt all alone and helpless.

I ran headlong into an old college classmate who stopped me in my tracks. She was a social worker at the hospital and could tell that I was more that a little distressed. She calmed me down as much as possible, and we talked. She definitely helped me settle down. I believe it was a godsend that she was there.

Becky survived. I don't know how. I was incredulous that they didn't sedate her but used nurses to restrain her as if she were a wild animal. I couldn't believe that they wouldn't allow me to be with her. I am sure had I been there we could have worked it out without the ensuing trauma. For years after that she hated going to the doctor. She was wary of anyone wearing a white coat. She especially hated going to the hospital. Again, the guilt was overwhelming. Why my daughter? Why this test? Why? Why? Why?

Becky's chromosomes were perfectly normal. The doctors could only conclude one thing; it was a congenital birth injury caused by the trauma of the forceps delivery and the aftereffects of the spinal block being given in haste and stopping labor, and the resultant deprivation of oxygen.

The Conference and Diagnosis

After all the testing results were compiled and computed, a conference was held with all the staff members involved in the evaluation. Both parents were required to be in attendance. During the conference I was given the distinct impression that they thought we were also a little slow. Who else would have a child with delayed development except slow parents? The analogies they gave us were so demeaning. I tried at one point to rebut a statement and was told something inane about catching the golden ring on the merry-go-round. "You know, not everyone can catch it, don't you, Mrs. Meyers?"

The doctor in charge was the coldest, most calculating woman I have ever encountered. It was like she was carved out of marble. The staff's archaic attitude and stereotyping of Becky was infuriating. Statements like "she will never be able to distinguish right from wrong", and "when she throws her temper tantrums I want you to put her in a dark closet and shut the door" enraged me. I became equally as furious when they wouldn't let me contradict what they were saying. In other words, my being Becky's mother and living with her twenty-four hours a day did not count for anything. How could I possibly know my own child? I was just her mother, so they stated. They not only stereotyped the children they evaluated, but they put their parents in a pigeonhole, too.

Luckily, they did not recommend an institution. They felt she would be fine at home. My goal was to keep her at home, make her a part of the family in every way and raise her the best way I knew how, with normalcy and acceptance. Of course, had she been a threat to herself or to her siblings, an institution might have been the only answer. We considered ourselves very lucky that she was so agreeable and easy going.

The final diagnosis, based on the testing and her delivery records from Penrose Hospital, was hypoxia or anoxia, lack of oxygen during delivery. The doctor, in his haste to get the delivery accomplished, applied the spinal too early and stopped labor. The time spent in the birth canal without oxygen caused her defects. The global effects of the oxygen deficit were very obvious in her EEG and other tests. She did not have a spike in any area; she was at the same level in all areas of her brain function. Results of that nature indicate a general lack of oxygen at delivery or at the time of trauma. Thank God she was delivered when she was. Another 30 seconds in the birth canal and she might have been a vegetable. I had grounds for a lawsuit, but knew that such action would not make her better, and it was not our nature to sue anyone, anyway.

Having that philosophy about litigation did not eliminate the what-ifs. Oh, if only my doctor had not been out of town. He was a personal friend and would not have hurried the process for his own benefit. I have learned since, however, that those two doctors produced many children like Becky for the same reasons and by the same miscalculation. They dreaded hearing women scream and moan during the delivery process, so they recommended spinals to deaden the birth canal and eliminate any pain. In retrospect, spinals didn't really prevent much pain. If applied appropriately, the baby's head should be crowning. The labor process is then far enough along that the mother can keep the pushing going. The final stages of delivery are minutes long at the most. By the time the baby's head has crowned the labor pains are almost a faint memory. Thank God doctors have been forced by women and society to change their procedures, and thank God so many more women are becoming doctors. Natural birth is the way to go, if possible. These two doctors really didn't care about their patients as individual persons with feelings and needs. Money was their bottom line and don't discount their own personal comfort level.

We tried not to spend time on "what if" and "if only." Becky is a delight in her own way and has changed the lives and thoughts of many people. She is a contributor. Read on and find out more about her.

The Trike

Once she walked she just <u>had</u> to learn to ride a tricycle. I went to the Salvation Army Store and found a used trike that was just the right size for a two-year-old. It was the walking exercise all over again, only this time it was putting her feet on the pedals and turning the wheel. She just looked at me. She made no effort to try to push or move the wheel under her own power. I was patience personified, and we worked day after day, week after week. No progress!

Realizing that she would do this in her time and in her own way, I finally put the tricycle away until a future time.

In the summer of 1964 her father was hired as the head track coach at Colorado State University in Fort Collins, Colorado. In August 1964 we moved to that college town and lived in married student housing. His hiring was so late in the school year that we couldn't find other accommodations.

Married student housing consisted of two story apartment buildings facing each other over a two-block distance with a laundry house at the north end. There were probably ten sets of buildings, called quads, in total. The inner yard was a perfect place for children to play, grass covered and lined with sidewalks on all four sides, with no streets or parking lots to worry about.

We had only one car, which I was allowed to use one day a week. On the other days, I would load Becky and Cindy into a little red wagon and we would head out to explore our new surroundings. We got to know our neighborhood quite well, especially the Dairy Queen, and folks knew us by the little red wagon and the friendly little girls being pulled in it.

One day, in the early spring, after the weather had warmed up, I stepped outside my front door to check on the girls. Becky was nowhere in sight. I asked a group of women standing about if any of them had seen her. One of them piped up and said, "Yeah, I just saw her riding a tricycle toward the laundry house."

I chuckled and said, "That couldn't have been Becky. She can't ride a trike."

"Oh yeah? Who is it then?" she asked, pointing toward that end of the quad. I couldn't believe my eyes. There was Becky pedaling as fast as she could down the sidewalk. We had given up trying to teach her months ago. Just like walking, she just decided on the spur of the moment to do it, and do it she did. The tricycle became her main means of mobilization after that. Who knows what triggered that undertaking? Was it a

Becky on trike with siblings

more efficient form of transportation? Was it peer pressure? Was it just her time frame? We will never know.

Plum and Daisy

In August 1965, I discovered I was pregnant again. It was our first planned pregnancy. Having delivered Cindy, who had been a routine delivery, I knew not to worry about having another special child. Besides, this one might be a boy!

Becky

Looking at our little apartment and considering the fact that we were not really married students, we decided to find a more appropriate home for our growing family. We found a neat, clean little house at the corner of Plum and Daisy Streets on the west side of Fort Collins. It had a basement apartment, which we could rent out, a big kitchen area, two large bedrooms, a laundry room and a single bathroom. It would do for a little while.

The girls continued to grow and develop. They found friends in the neighborhood and life seemed normal. I grew, as pregnant women do, and felt so fortunate to have two little girls who could play so well and be so independent. I was nauseous for about five months and had difficulty being up and about. I relied on the girls to watch one another and report in to me on a regular basis, though they were never outside alone unless they were in the back yard, which was fenced. Pretty high expectations for a three and four year old. They were great, and, as I've mentioned before, Becky *did* know the difference between right and wrong. She was also aware of safety issues and somehow knew when I needed to be warned.

One day I was melting some meat drippings in a pan. I wanted to pour them into a tin can and toss them in the incinerator once they had congealed. I turned on the burner and proceeded to sit at the table to write a letter. Becky was playing in the kitchen with her dolls. I became so engrossed in the letter that I forgot all about the fat on the stove.

Becky's words were not perfect, and when she wanted milk she asked for 'moke.' She came up to me, pulled my face toward her with her little hands, looked into my eyes and said, "Moke, Mommy, moke."

I asked her if she wanted milk.

"No, Mommy. Moke! Mommy, moke!" she responded.

I asked again if she wanted milk.

This time she took my hand and led me toward the stove saying, "Moke, Mommy, moke." At that instant the grease in the pan burst into flames. She was trying to tell me that there was 'smoke, Mommy, smoke'. I quickly, and not without a bit of panic, located the baking soda, turned off the burner and doused the burning drippings with the soda. The fire went out without further incident, but bless Becky for being so alert. This, my child who needs more consistent discipline and doesn't know right from wrong, who needs to be put in a dark closet when she has a temper tantrum. Please!

Retest

Time for a second evaluation. With dread I headed for Denver. Don decided he would not go this year. I left Cindy with a neighbor and planned to be in Denver for the whole day. This time the testing was not so terrifying for Becky; they didn't need to perform the physical exams, just the psychological. They let me stay with her while she identified common objects and tried to put pegs in holes. I was not the least bit impressed with the psychologist. He was cold, calculating and took no interest in trying to befriend Becky. He was all business. I wondered again how such people get into the business of evaluating children. It seemed to me that one of the qualifications would be to like children.

She had difficulty recognizing some very common items, such as an airplane. She had never seen one on the ground, so it was not familiar to her. I must admit I did make excuses for her during that testing period. I was not in denial. After all, I was the first to suspect that something was skewed with her development. I just wanted her to perform way beyond his expectations. It didn't happen.

After lunch I was called into another staffing. They proceeded to give me the news that Becky was indeed developmentally delayed, and even farther behind her age group this year than she had been the year before. Again there were the perennial platitudes; the stereotyping of parents and child; the coldness and the indifference, ad nauseam. After all, who really cares about a child who will not be able to contribute to the betterment of society or learn how to function normally in this life?

Their parting advice was threefold: 1) work on toilet training, 2) look for a pre-school for her to attend, and 3) practice more consistent discipline. After all, this was a child who would never know right from wrong.

As I was leaving the conference room, the obsequious social worker tapped me on the shoulder and said, "Now you know, Mrs. Meyers, you cannot hold your normal children back because Becky can't keep up with them."

I pivoted on my heel, looked her straight in the eye and said with the steeliest voice I could muster, "For your information, I turn Becky loose to try to keep up with them." Doing an about face, I stormed down the hall and out to the parking lot. I was churning inside. What a stupid woman! What did she know about what happened on a weekly basis in our home? She was making assumptions based on what, I didn't know, but certainly not on our family's day-to-day existence. I wasn't sure how much more of this I could take.

I did remember their recommendations as we headed back to Fort Collins. I was seething all the way home. When I returned home, I gave her father my impression of the whole experience. He took it all with a grain of salt. Nothing seemed to bother him about the whole process. He didn't find it demeaning. My true sense is he didn't listen and he really didn't care. He had more important things to think about, like whether or not his team was going to win the next track meet. I think he perceived me as the typical hysterical female, and he chose to leave it all up to me.

A few days later I began the process of following up on their suggestions. Becoming successful at using the toilet regularly would only happen when Becky was ready. My intuition told me that would be like walking and riding the trike. One day she would just decide to do it and it would be done. I didn't want to push it for many reasons, the biggest being the emotional overlay it could cause.

I also didn't feel a need to become more consistent in my discipline. Becky did not require lots of discipline. For whatever reason, she was an obedient child who did not create havoc or get into mischief. I tried to become more aware of her behavior in general, in case I was just fooling myself into believing that she was a good girl. She was just a good girl. No need for special tactics or techniques to inspire good behavior. She just behaved well.

I did look into preschools. Most of the regular preschools in that day were not interested in participants who were not toilet trained. I called several and could not find one that was willing to take her. I did not give up on the idea, but did table it until after her brother was born.

On April 12, 1966, I put the girls to bed about 7:30 and went to my bowling league. I had overnight bags packed for them in case I went into labor at any time. Family friends were going to keep them for us for the five days I would be in the hospital. I only kept score at the bowling alley, having given up actually rolling a ball about two weeks prior. I came home with a neighbor who bowled in the same league, and we sat and talked for a while.

Suddenly, I felt a familiar twinge. Excusing myself, I went into the house about 11:00. I decided to shower, wash and set my hair, pack my overnight bag and then time the contractions. No sooner had I settled myself at the kitchen table than the contractions were four minutes apart and a minute in duration. I gently woke the girls, got them in the car and then woke their father. He said, as we backed down the driveway, "I hope you spit this one out in about forty-five minutes so I can come home and get a good night's sleep." A very sensitive man, he.

I let him down. Todd came in an hour and a half. They didn't even have time to prep me. He weighed nine pounds and three ounces, a big baby boy. We were so thrilled to have a son after two daughters. I could hardly wait to get him home. I would have been just as happy with another girl, but a boy was more than welcomed into our family.

Baylor Street

One of the football coaches at Colorado State University was leaving the staff in the summer of 1966 to take another job, and his house was for sale. We looked at it, day dreamed about it, and then, thanks to a loan from my mother-in-law, were able to purchase it. It was a bi-level house with white walls and royal blue carpeting. It had three bedrooms, one for the girls, one for Todd and a master bedroom for us. It was more than I had ever dreamed of having in my lifetime, though, in retrospect, it was just a tract home in a little subdivision.

I loved that the kids had their own room. I loved having a family room downstairs where the mess made by toys and playtime could not be seen by everyone. I loved having my own washer and dryer. And I loved being a mother to my three children.

When we moved, Todd was just three months old. There I was with three kids under the age of five moving into a house, nursing an infant and trying to handle all the household responsibilities. I was a very strong woman and quite well-organized. Before long everything was in its place, the yard was mowed and trimmed, and the kids were established in the neighborhood.

I realized I had to continue looking for a pre-school for Becky. The wife of my husband's supervisor had been a kindergarten teacher. She came to the house one day, observed Becky, and told me she saw no reason why Becky couldn't go to kindergarten. Regular kindergarten! That thought had never entered my mind. I took her word for it and began the process of getting Becky registered for the neighborhood kindergarten class. I was so excited about the prospect.

Becky ready for kindergarten

The schools did not hesitate to register her, and, on the first day of school, she entered the kindergarten class that was being held in a nearby church due to lack of space at the elementary school. I dressed her up just like a schoolgirl and proudly left her there after introducing her to the teacher. I could hardly wait to pick her up after school to see how her first day went.

To my dismay, she ran sobbing into my arms. She'd had a horrible experience. I never got details, but I did find out that the teacher could not tolerate any challenged student, regardless of intellect. Becky's developmental delays were not acceptable to this woman, and she treated her accordingly.

One day was all we gave that effort. I was not about to put her through that kind of misery more than once. Sadness for Becky's distress and a deep-seated anger aimed at the teacher ate at my inner being, but I had no recourse unless I wanted to fight the school district. It was not worth having Becky hurt again to prove a point. We started searching for other alternatives.

Fort Collins had an Easter Seal School. I made an appointment for an interview. On the day of the meeting at the school I dressed Becky in her best school clothes, bundled her brother in his infant seat, put Cindy in her car seat and headed for the Easter Seal Center. There a teacher talked to me with Becky close by. Cindy was into everything. This gentleman looked at me and asked, "Can't you do something about her?"

I shrugged my shoulders and told him that Cindy's behavior was considered 'normal' for a three year old. Maybe he didn't work with many 'normal' children and expected all of them to sit quietly. Becky was her usual cooperative and pleasant self. Would that she had been as 'busy' as her sister.

Becky was accepted as a student at the school, and I became immersed in the parents' organization. She flourished with teachers who understood her limitations, brought out her strengths and had the patience required to work with a variety of special students. I was so glad to see her loving school.

It was in this fifth year of Becky's life that she began to use the toilet effectively for urination, at least during the daylight hours. She still required protection during the night. Whether it was the brain damage, her lack of motivation, or my enabling her will never be known, but bedwetting followed her until she moved into a group home at age 22.

Third Time's a Charm?

A phone call and a message about the third evaluation session were received in October 1966. I was told that my husband would have to come to the staff conference because I had not followed through on the recommendations from the prior year. I came unglued. I fumed all the way to Denver. How dare they imply that I was not capable of following through with recommendations for my child? I could hardly wait to confront the social worker, who had been the one to pass along that admonishment.

Her father was reluctant to attend, but believed it would be best for Becky if he came. His interpretation of and reactions to the information dispensed by the so-called experts were always different from mine. I felt his presence was not only unnecessary, but a detriment to communication. His mind was always on his job, not in the here and now. His presence would certainly not assure that I could follow through on their recommendations; I had already done so.

We sat through the evaluation listening to the same drivel and misinformation. They even had the gall to bring up birth control for Becky. She was all of five years old! Who thinks about such things at that tender young age?

With anger and tension in my voice I enumerated for those at the table the steps taken to get Becky into school. I informed them that she was using the toilet consistently during the day and that disciplining her to the extent they suggested was unnecessary and inhumane. The meeting came to an end and I stormed out of the room in pursuit of the social worker.

I cornered her in the hallway and, getting in her face, I let her know I did not appreciate her accusations about my alleged inability or unwillingness to support their recommendations. I again emphasized the fact that all of the suggestions were taken seriously and acted upon.

In a condescending manner she informed me, "That was our means of making sure your husband would come." It was only a ploy to get my husband there! Never mind that it was insulting and denigrating to me. They had never treated me like the intelligent, informed, educated woman that I was. The implication from day one was that I, too, must be 'retarded' in order to have a 'retarded' child. Here it was raising its ugly head again.

As we maneuvered through the Denver traffic I was livid. I made an on the spot decision that we would not return to Children's Hospital for another evaluation, ever! I knew that The University of Colorado's Medical Center also had an evaluation clinic for children with developmental disabilities. I was determined to have Becky's records transferred to that facility. Our pediatrician had done his internship in that very clinic, so how could it be anything but better than Children's cold, dark-ages attitude toward children like Becky?

I made inquiries at Colorado General Hospital, as it was known then, and was told that they would not duplicate the work that had been done at Children's. I was discouraged, but not defeated. After we moved back to Boulder, I decided she would be evaluated annually at the Boulder County Developmental Disabilities Center (BCBDD). She would be a client of that entity in a few short years, and it made sense in every way. She was accepted into their evaluation program without hesitation. What a relief to know that I didn't have to face those people at Children's Hospital again.

After that last miserable experience at the Children's Hospital, Becky's evaluations were so routine that I have no distinct memory of them, except for one. I mentioned previously that Children's Hospital wanted to talk about birth control when she was five. Well, during her twelve-year-old evaluation I was the one who brought up birth control.

My concern lay in the fact that the birth control pill was contraindicated for her due to its side effects. I was asking for suggestions to be used in the future if the need arose. Dr. Takahashi, our former pediatrician, had become the medical director for the BCBDD and was presiding at this evaluation. He glanced my way and then said, "Why are you worried? There is nothing to indicate that Becky would have a retarded child."

I was incredulous. That statement just reinforced the righteousness of my changing doctors all those many years ago. I replied to him, "That is exactly my concern. Do you really think she could raise a 'normal' child?" I had observed developmentally delayed parents with very bright children trying to discipline, educate and care for them, and not with much success. I didn't want to take that chance, nor did I relish the idea of raising my grandchildren.

After a few years her school's annual 'Individual Education Plan' sufficed for the annual evaluations, and formal evaluations became a thing of the past. What a relief!!

Bladder Infections

Soon after we moved to Fort Collins, Becky began to have chronic bladder infections. The question arose as to the cause of this problem. How much of it could be attributed to the brain damage at birth and how much to some problem with her personal hygiene? Every six weeks or so I whisked her off to Dr. Humphrey's office where he would examine a urine sample, prescribe a sulfa drug and send us home with specific instructions regarding amount of fluids required and information on bathing and clothing little girls.

This went on for three years. I dutifully took her to the doctor every time the symptoms were obvious, and every time the treatment was the same. I thought I was doing the best thing for my child until the day in July 1967, when Dr. Humphrey's new associate, Dr. Burke, was scheduled to see her. As the new doctor in the office, he had fewer patients and thus more time to study her medical history. When it was discovered that she had, yet again, another bladder infection, he warned me:

"Mrs. Meyers, do you know how many bladder infections Becky has had in the last three years?" he asked with impatience.

"Of course, I do. I bring her in every time she gets one."

"Well," he continued. "We worry when a little boy gets *one* bladder infection and we worry when a little girl gets a *second*, and this child has had more than I can count. Before long they will begin to affect her kidneys, if they haven't already."

I didn't know how to respond. Dr. Humphrey had never said anything like this. He must have been so busy with so many patients he couldn't remember from one visit to another why we were there. He probably never took the time to review her chart the way Dr. Burke had.

I was told to get her to a specialist as soon as possible. I informed him that we would be moving in a few weeks to Boulder, Colorado. He emphasized the importance of getting her to a urologist as soon as we were settled in our new home. I truly believe the man saved us tremendous medical expenses and possibly saved Becky's life.

At the earliest possible moment after moving I contacted Dr. Poynter, the urologist at the Boulder Medical Center and requested a complete workup for Becky. It seems that the stagnant urine had already backed up enough to adversely affect the ureters, the tubes that connect the kidneys to the bladder. Her holding urine so long in her bladder before relieving the pressure caused her bladder to stretch and pull until it resembled the bladder of a "seventy-five year old man". Since the urine had nowhere to go it affected the ureters making them soft and floppy, until they could not shut off the flow to the kidneys. Old, stagnant urine was backing up into her kidneys. It wouldn't be long until the kidneys would suffer irreparable damage. We caught it just in time. The kidneys were still clear, but not for long, unless something were done to correct the problem.

She was scheduled for a bilateral re-implantation of the ureters. In this surgical procedure the urologist detaches the ureters from the bladder, removes the affected portion, and then inserts them back into the bladder exposing only fresh tissue to the urine. The system is quite primitive, involving a kinking process that prevents the urine from backing up into the kidneys. When that tissue gets soft and mushy it loses its elasticity and can no longer kink, thus allowing the urine into the kidneys, where it does not belong. Add to that bacteria from an infection, and severe kidney problems are in the offing.

Sounds simple enough, doesn't it? Becky came through the surgery like a champ; it was the recovery that was so difficult. She laid in her bed with tubes coming out of her little body in three places. A tube protruding from her belly was filling a gallon jug with fluids from her bladder. Two tubes attached to bags hanging from the bedrails were draining her kidneys. She was so little to have all that baggage hanging from her body. The proverbial third day after surgery was the worst. She was writhing with pain and rolling from one side of the bed to the other, crying out. I was trying to comfort her and, at the same time, keep all the bottles, bags and tubes intact. I decided at that point that she would never go through anything like this again unless it were a matter of life and death.

After it was all behind us, it was the best thing we could have done. She has had only one bladder infection in forty-one years. She wears cotton panties and takes only showers. We found out through all this that bathing in bubble bath is highly likely to cause bladder infections in girls. We will never know why she had so many bladder infections, but thanks to modern medicine we were able to take care of it in time.

Washington School with Mrs. Woodrum and Ms. Walker

We moved back to Boulder when Becky was six years old, the summer of 1967. Don had been hired as the head track coach at the University of Colorado. Again, I was faced with the dilemma of finding an appropriate school situation for her. Boulder, Colorado, was always on the cutting edge when it came to special education, so it was just a matter of registering her in the best program to meet her needs. She was still considered "educable" at this age, so off to school she went. She began her public school education at Washington School in north Boulder with Mrs. Marjorie Woodrum, an incredibly insightful, gentle, older woman whose heart was huge and her arms long enough to embrace every child in her classroom at the same time.

Becky flourished with this woman as her teacher. She was so happy and self-confident. My only request of Mrs. Woodrum was that she not put undue stress on Becky with expectations beyond her abilities. I was more focused on Becky's being happy than her being the smartest child in the class. I was criticized for that attitude but have never regretted it. I believe that Becky is who she is today because she was accepted for her limitations and her abilities and not pressured to perform beyond those abilities.

The class was equivalent to kindergarten and met for a half day. I taught elementary school Spanish at two of the primary schools in the mornings after dropping Don at the University, Becky off at school, leaving Cindy at pre-school and Todd with babysitters. I would begin my pickup rounds after my teaching was finished for the day. Cindy was four years old and in the Boulder Preschool, which was about four blocks from Becky's school. I had found two elderly sisters to take care of Todd, who was sixteen months old when the school year began. Their home was on the north side of Boulder, also. The school district was very cooperative and picked Becky up at school and dropped her at the sisters' home. I would leave my last school,; pick up Cindy, then Becky and Todd and home we would go.

Our afternoons included trips on the city bus system, playing at local parks, and grocery shopping. We had but one car, so we would head for the University about five o'clock to pick up their father. While I jogged around the field house, the children played in the long jump pit or jumped on the landing platform for the pole vault. Everything seemed to fall into place. It seemed like moving back to Boulder was a good thing for our family. The children flourished that year both at home and away from home.

Self -Defense on the School Bus

Summer came and went and Becky started her second year of school. She had graduated from Mrs. Woodrum's class and had moved on to Miss Walker's. Miss Walker had a different approach to teaching, and Becky developed nicely under her tutelage also. We were becoming aware that Becky was very adaptable, an unusual quality for children who are developmentally delayed. She didn't mind the long ride on the bus. New teachers and new children in the class didn't bother her. She just adjusted.

After the school year was well under way, we noticed Becky becoming hesitant to get on the bus. We pondered the reasons why with no answers until Miss Walker informed us that two higher functioning boys who rode Becky's bus decided it would be fun to tease her. They would take her hat, mittens or lunch box and play keep away with them. Becky was never an aggressive child nor had anyone ever treated her this way; she had no clue how to counteract their harassment.

Because I had determined years ago that Becky would dress like her peers, have all the benefits her peers enjoyed and be as normal in those aspects as possible, she went to school everyday looking like a schoolgirl. She wore skirts and sweaters, dresses, jumpers and blouses, color-coordinated and in style. She always looked cute and so girlish. Miss Walker suggested, based on her own experiences as a child, that I dress Becky in jeans and sweatshirts in hopes of discouraging these two young men from picking on her. I was willing to oblige; if it would work it was worth a try.

Within a week of changing Becky's attire, she hauled off and clobbered both boys, and they never bothered her again. She has only worn a dress or skirt four or five times since then, for weddings, baptisms and funerals. She has no desire to look like a female. Jeans and tee shirts, sweats and athletic jackets are her usual attire to this day.

Off to Aurora 7 Elementary

Becky turned eight and was going to attend the same school that fall as her sister Cindy. Aurora 7 Elementary School was within walking distance of our home. I was excited about the prospect of her gaining a degree of independence walking to and from school with her sister. Her teacher was a gentle, soft-spoken lady with a big smile and a bigger heart. Her name was Grace Wells, and she literally fell in love with Becky. It was hard not to. Becky was well-behaved, happy, cute as a bug and loved going to school.

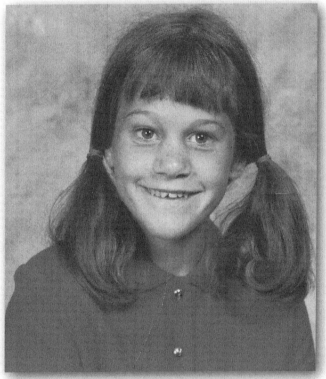

Becky at Aurora 7, age 8

At the first parent-teacher conference Mrs. Wells reported that, upon arrival at school each morning, Becky would burst through the door and say with exuberance, "Look who's here!!" She had the positive self-image every child should have. I do believe she was born with it. I cannot remember when she wasn't happy and smiling and loving life, as simple as it was for her.

Each parent-teacher conference thereafter was a very encouraging experience for me. Mrs. Wells had nothing but praise for Becky's progress and her general attitude toward school and her classmates.

About six weeks into the school year Becky and Cindy did not come home at the usual time. Just as I was about to check into the situation the phone rang. The school's secretary asked why Becky had not yet been picked up. Grabbing my keys, I muttered something into the phone and drove like a mad woman to the school. Becky was sitting patiently in the office waiting for me to arrive. Cindy was nowhere around.

Sick with worry, I began calling all her friends' homes. Sure enough, she was playing with one of her friends and had completely forgotten to walk Becky home. She was all of six years old. Instead of being angry with her, I did some in-depth thinking and realized that I had put a huge burden of responsibility on a mere six year old. Of course, she would rather play with her friends than walk her big sister home. I did require that she let me know when she was planning to go to a friend's house after school.

We talked about the situation, and the decision was made for Becky to ride the Special Education bus to and from the school. How much more realistic that decision was for all of us. It relieved me of future worry and freed Cindy to be a regular little six-year-old girl.

Becky was retained in Mrs. Wells' classroom the following year. She did not move on as did so many of the others in the class. As the room mother for her class, I had the opportunity to spend a bit of time in the classroom observing academics and social interaction. Midway through her second year with Mrs. Wells, I began to notice that Becky was head and shoulders above the other students, and most of those from her first year at Aurora 7 had moved up to the next level. I only noticed, I didn't speak out. I loved having Becky so close to home, and I loved the fact that Mrs. Wells thought she was so special. It never entered my mind that we were not being fair to her.

In the spring of that year Mrs. Wells had to have emergency surgery and called in a substitute, a woman named Martha Truhlahr. Since Mrs. Truhlahr was not personally involved with Becky, she could be much more objective about her placement in this particular classroom. After teaching and observing for two weeks, she recommended that Becky be moved to the 'trainable' center, North Broadway School, the following year. A staffing was scheduled and invitations were sent out to all those involved.

I arrived at the school, found the conference room and was greeted by a huge table surrounded with every conceivable person who had ever worked with Becky in the school system. The school psychologist was there, as were the physical education teacher, Mrs. Wells, Mrs. Truhlahr, the director of Special Education, a speech therapist, the principal, and on and on. I was a bit overwhelmed to say the least. As each person had his/her say, I paid close attention to the spoken words. Little did they know that I was silently in agreement, having observed the differences between Becky and her classmates. I listened carefully as they struggled to convince me that North Broadway School was the most appropriate setting for Becky. They cajoled and persuaded and simpered. Being a realist, it was no surprise to me. Apparently they had unpleasant experiences with many parents who were adamant about their children not attending North Broadway School. Parents of that ilk believed it put a blight on the family name; a real sign of failure if a child could not stay in the public school system. I only wanted what was best for Becky, and it was obvious that Aurora 7 was not the school for her.

When I nodded in agreement, had no arguments and asked what the procedure would be to enroll her the next fall, they almost fell out of their chairs. It was comical to watch. They had such looks of complete relief on their faces. They had no idea who I was or how I thought. As in so many other conferences involving my daughter, I was stereotyped, and plans were made accordingly. What a surprise it was to them that I would be so acquiescent.

The Brownie Scouts

While attending Aurora 7 Elementary School, Becky became a Brownie Scout with her sister, Cindy. It was easy for her to be accepted into the troop because I was a co-leader. Diana Schwartzwelter was the other leader, and she had no qualms whatsoever with the idea of Becky being part of the group. After all, Brownies are just little girls learning about scouting at a very primary level.

Being a Brownie Scout did require, however, learning the Girl Scout Promise, "On my honor I will try to do my duty to God and my country, to help other people at all times and to obey the Girl Scout law." Diana gave me permission to prompt Becky at the investiture ceremony, so we spent many hours repeating the Promise at home and in the car. The big day arrived and Becky was all dressed up in her Brownie uniform. One at a time the girls repeated the Promise with the proper salute, and then it was Becky's turn. She raised her arm with two fingers held high, and I gave her the first two words. Off she went, completely on her own, and recited the Promise verbatim without hesitation. All the parents in attendance were in tears. It was such an achievement for her and one I never thought she could accomplish. She showed me a thing or two, and it wouldn't be the last time.

Accident Prone

Becky loves cats. One of the first cats we owned was a gray tabby named Tiger. When she got the cat in her clutches she didn't let go. The cat had to have a lot of patience to put up with her attention.

One day she was holding Tiger in her deathlike grip and she tripped. Instead of letting the cat go and catching herself, she hung on to him for dear life and hit the doorframe with her head. The blood spurted everywhere. She had split her forehead open. The laceration was about an inch and a quarter long and, by my estimation required a trip to the doctor for stitches.

It was a Saturday night about 6:00 when we arrived at the Boulder Medical Center. Dr. Aumiller was the only pediatrician on duty, and he was not our regular doctor. He reluctantly examined her and then asked the nurse to bring him a butterfly bandage.

Now, I must make you aware that Becky constantly wrinkled her forehead. There was no way a butterfly bandage was going to hold that wound together. I asked him point blank if he were planning to simply put a butterfly on the wound. His response was positive.

I said, "I want it stitched."

Through gritted teeth and with much chagrin he told his nurse to bring him the suture tray. He then proceeded to take his frustration out on my child. He poked the needle in then yanked it through her skin with his forceps. He repeated this torture until the entire wound was stitched. I glared at him throughout the procedure. So what if it was 6:00 on a Saturday night? He was a doctor, for crying out loud, and his job was to take care of patients and do so with a little compassion.

It was our fate to run into him a couple of years later under another emergency situation, and, again, he showed his true colors.

Brain Injury on Top of Brain Injury

My half sister, Susan, was getting married in Montgomery, Alabama, in late summer, 1970. We had plans to attend the wedding and were driving to Alabama with my sister and her family. Our plans involved renting a large van and driving leisurely through the South, stopping along the way to take in the history and the landscape. I had just finished my summer job at the local swimming pool and was busily cleaning and getting packed for the trip. It was a Saturday, and Becky was next door playing with her little friend, Jody. Becky was nine and Jody was three, and they were cozy as a caterpillar in a cocoon, best of friends.

I'll never forget the day the two of them were out playing in the yard, taking turns pulling one another in a wagon. They were alternating the roles of mother and child. Initially Becky was the mother and Jody was the child and the usual child/parent banter could be overheard. Then they changed places. Becky climbed in the wagon and Jody became the mother figure. Jody said, "Okay, Becky, now you're the baby."

And Becky replied with a big smile, "Yeah, and I'm retarded."

Had we gone overboard trying to make her feel accepted just as she was? Alas, I digress.

Back to Saturday and the wedding trip: Dust was flying in the garage as I swept it vigorously. My neighbor Dal, Jody's father, walked through the cloud of dust with a most serious look on his face and said, "I think you better come to our house, Holly. Becky has fallen."

Now, Becky's birth injury came with balance problems and mild diplegia and falling was nothing new. She often tripped and fell head-long onto the sidewalk or into the dirt. Her hands and knees were per-petually scraped and bruised. It was just a way of life and an everyday expectation. I knew from the look on Dal's face this was different. I dropped the broom and ran to their back door. Bursting through the door, I saw his wife, Judy, on the phone. She was as pale as her white walls and had a sense of urgency in her voice.

"Where is Becky," I demanded to know.

"She's down the basement. I'm calling an ambleance (sic)", she responded in a frantic voice.

I bounded down the steps two or three at a time, hardly noticing whether my feet were touching them or not. There lay my child, face-down on the concrete floor, lying still as a fallen log in the forest. She did not move or blink an eye. She was unconscious, out cold. Like a fool, in my panic, I turned her over and picked her up, all my first aid train-ing going up in smoke. I yelled for Dal to get the car and started up the stairs with her.

"Don't you want to wait for the ambleance?" Judy asked.

"I can't wait for an ambulance. We have to go **NOW**!" I shouted in response.

Dal had the car running, and I climbed into the back seat as carefully as I could. I laid her head on my lap and tried to make her as comfortable and safe as possible.

Dal backed out of the driveway and headed toward town. I was praying and the words were coming out as fast as I could process them in my distraught state. Looking at her little body lying there motionless, with scabs and scratches and bruises from her many tumbles to the ground, I just prayed that we would get there in time and that the medical staff would believe that she had fallen. Oh, the thoughts that went through my head.

"The light is red. What shall I do?" Dal asked.

"Run it," I demanded. "I will pay for the ticket."

Run it he did with a Sheriff in hot pursuit. With red lights flashing the sheriff pulled us over. As soon as Dal rolled down the window I shouted, "Will you please help us get to the hospital? My daughter fell and is unconscious."

He ordered us to follow him, jumped back in his vehicle, turned on his siren and led us to the emergency room without a hitch. What a blessing!!!

She was put into a patient room following an examination in the emergency room. Our regular pediatrician was not available, so his associate, Dr. Aumiller, the compassionate applier of stitches, was called in. I must admit I was hysterical. I asked him several times when he thought she would regain consciousness. He finally looked at me and said, "Why don't you just go home. The last thing we need here is a hysterical mother." I defied him and stayed, and stayed and stayed. I would not leave her side. I couldn't believe that, once again, I was forced to deal with this doctor, he with no empathy or compassion. I determined that if he were the only pediatrician on call in the future I would settle for the family physician in their practice. No more Dr. Aumiller for me.

I settled in to stay with her for as long as necessary. Our travel plans were cancelled, and the long wait began. She waxed in and out of consciousness for about four days. She would waken, reach for a stuffed monkey that was given her by friends of the family, and then fade back into an unconscious state. Our regular pediatrician was monitoring her very closely and, after the fourth day, informed us that we needed to take her to Colorado General Hospital (CGH), now known as Colorado University Medical Center. Through X-rays he had found fluid on her brain and thought she might possibly need a shunt to drain the fluid. He was uncertain whether the fluid was there from birth or had developed from this recent injury.

An ambulance took her to Colorado General Hospital, and we followed in our car. She was admitted to a regular room for about two days, and, when she didn't come out of the coma, was placed in ICU. During her ten-day stay at CGH she was given every test possible. No sooner would she finish one test and fall asleep than they would drag her off for another examination. Her kidneys were functioning normally, her heart and lungs were normal, her EEG showed no abnormal swelling, and the testing just went on and on. She was put back on the pediatric floor after three days in ICU, but not without more prying and poking. After six days I decided "No more!" Enough is enough! I parked myself outside her room, and, had I a shotgun, I would have laid it across my lap and dared anyone to disturb her. No one did. Wonder of wonders. It's just as well. I probably would have been arrested and sent to jail. As it turned out the last possible test had been run, and she was resting quietly in her bed.

I checked on her periodically, and after about two hours she woke up. I mean she woke up! She called me 'Mommy'; she was alert; she was one hundred percent there. She knew her name and asked where she was. I noticed that her hands were terribly shaky. No one could tell me why that was happening, but they shook as if she had tremors and was upset about something. She could not control the shaking.

I left for a few minutes, crossed the street and bought her a music box, a 'Kitty in the Barrels' toy, which had five decreasingly smaller barrels with a kitty in the smallest one, and a puzzle. I felt she needed something to keep her hands busy. What I bought was just the ticket. She wound the music box endlessly and put the barrels together and took them apart over and over and over again, and the puzzle pieces were ragged by the time she was discharged.

Two days later we took her home. She was our old Becky. For all intents and purposes one would never know that she had just been through a traumatic experience. The injury did not exacerbate her original birth injury. What an answer to prayer! What a miracle! At the time I was unaware of the effects of serious brain injury on the personality and behavior of the injured party. I think it was a blessing that I didn't know. I probably would have been a basket case.

The only behavioral change we noticed was an unexplained, quite noticeable possessiveness regarding her personal belongings. It was sort of like she knew she almost didn't come back and didn't want to take any chances on losing those things again. Who knows how her mind works? I am thankful that she did not have any serious residual effects from the fall.

The next year of school at Aurora 7 was without incident. Upon informing her teacher of the accident, I warned her to look for changes in Becky's behavior and abilities. None were reported.

North Broadway School, Here We Come

It was time to look into a new school. As I mentioned earlier in the book, Becky was very adaptable to change. A new school was not to shake that ability to accept new things. She was ten years old in 1971, the year we registered her at North Broadway School. The school was bright and cheery, with a huge arboretum in the center of the atrium. Avocado trees reached for the sun that shone through a large skylight and other tropical plants wound their way around the trunks of the trees and cascaded over the stone wall that surrounded the garden. Classrooms surrounded the atrium and a smiling secretary sat at a desk near the entrance. Therapeutic equipment was lying about on the floor, and the walls were covered with art projects the students had made in summer school. It looked warm and welcoming.

I was filling out the paper work I had been given by the secretary when I noticed a stocky woman walking down the hallway. I had first seen her while playing women's flag football in a city recreation league. She was one tough broad. I couldn't imagine what she was doing there. I asked the secretary who she was.

"Oh, that's Barb Shore. She's our PE teacher."

"I am not sure I want my daughter in this school if _she_ is going to be her PE teacher," I said.

Becky with Barb Shore

"Oh, she is wonderful with the students. You can't believe what she gets them to do. You have nothing to fear," she replied to my motherly concerns.

She was so sincere I decided to have faith and let Becky take the plunge. That secretary was absolutely correct in her appraisal of Barb. Barb was not only the physical education teacher; she was the Area Coordinator for Special Olympics. She was one fantastic lady, and she worked miracles with her students.

North Broadway School was a school for 'trainable' children and teens and was managed by an entity called the Boulder County Board for Developmental Disabilities, a part of the Colorado Department of Institutions, now known as Imagine. The Department of Education had nothing to do with the oversight of the program, thus many of the teachers were not certified in special education or even had their teaching degrees for that matter. Regardless, they were the most dedicated, talented, involved staff of teachers I have ever had the privilege of knowing.

Before long Barbara Shore had Becky turning flips on the trampoline. Granted, they were from a sitting position, but beyond my belief until I saw it with my own two eyes. I had to ask Becky to do it again after I saw her do it the first time. She complied with a big grin on her face after she completed the trick.

Barb taught Becky to swim the breaststroke and the butterfly and helped her overcome her fear of deep water. Becky ran track and field for the Special Olympics and took home beaucoup medals every year at the competition. She eventually swam competitively for Special Olympics, also. Had she stayed in the public school program, I doubt she would have had the opportunities for learning and participation that she had at North Broadway School.

Oh, What a Beautiful Morning

In the spring of her first year at the school she came home and announced that she was singing a solo in the spring program.

"Sure you are, Becky," I responded, with a hint of disbelief in my voice.

"I really am, Mom, honest," she replied.

And honest she was. It was not just any solo, it was "Oh, What a Beautiful Morning" from <u>Oklahoma</u>. She sang on key, and the words were clear and easy to understand. I sat in my chair and wept tears of joy. Unfortunately, camcorders were not available at that time. I would love to have a video of her standing on the stage singing with such confidence and ability. She showed me a thing or two, again. Remember the Brownie pledge?

Her first music therapist at the school was a woman named TeeDee Donahue. She played guitar, made music fun and brought out the best in each student regardless of the extent of disability. Her music programs were delightful. I always questioned labeling these students 'trainable.' They were way beyond that classification!

Academics and Curriculum

Becky's first academic teacher at North Broadway School was a woman named Selma Altschuler. She and Becky were buddies. Becky blossomed in Selma's classroom and we were well pleased with the results. At the first teacher conference she seemed a little uptight and a bit standoffish. I began by telling her how pleased we were with Becky's progress and positive attitude about school. Her facial features relaxed and she let out a big breath and said, "Oh, thank God!"

Surprised, I asked her what that was all about. She informed me that she had dreaded the conference. As it turns out Mrs. Wells had written such glowing and unrealistic reports about Becky's abilities that Mrs. Altschuler thought that we would think her a failure as a teacher. She then informed us that Becky could do none of the things Mrs. Wells indicated she was capable of doing. It became very clear to us that Becky was in the right educational environment, finally.

Before Becky graduated from North Broadway School, she had been involved in Special Olympics, the choir, the bell choir, cheerleading and swimming, activities for which she would never have qualified in a public school.

Braces

About the same time Becky started attending North Broadway School, I noticed that she couldn't take a bite out of a sandwich. I held the sandwich for her and told her to bite and it came out basically intact, not even a tooth mark. I then asked her to put her teeth together and smile for me so I could see her teeth. Her front teeth did not meet at all. In fact, only the back two molars meshed together. No wonder she couldn't bite anything, at least not effectively. My children visited the dentist every year without fail. I have no idea why it was never mentioned or why I never noticed it myself.

Upon evaluation, it seemed that Becky had a severe malocclusion probably due to the negative effect of the brain injury on the development of the jaw and her habitual thumb sucking. In addition, the speech therapist at her school also determined that she was a 'tongue thruster'. When she swallowed drinks or food she would thrust her tongue between her teeth. A person who swallows normally keeps the tongue behind the teeth. The consensus was that the tongue thrusting had contributed significantly to the malocclusion.

Speech therapy was ordered and begun immediately. North Broadway School had a remarkable speech therapist. She later became a lawyer and helped me get legal guardianship of Becky. She diligently worked with Becky on the tongue thrusting which resulted in significant improvement. Once her swallow was relatively normal, we began consulting an orthodontist.

John Hayhurst, one of my classmates from high school, was practicing orthodontistry in Boulder, so we chose him knowing he would take a personal interest in her. He took a shine to Becky and was willing to put braces on at age eleven rather than wait until her teeth had matured. The inability to eat efficiently was his major concern.

A new process had just been approved, and he decided that it would work for Becky's situation. With this technique the teeth were pulled together in twenty-four hours! It involved putting braces on the teeth with minute hooks attached and placing specially designed rubber bands on the hooks, alternating from upper teeth to lower teeth in a zig-zag pattern. It would mean getting sustenance through a straw until the bands could be removed. It seemed plausible when he explained it, so we agreed to have it done.

Little did I know how painful it would be. Becky has a very high threshold of pain; seldom does she complain. This means of closing the gap was excruciating for her. She threw herself on the floor in the family room and writhed in pain for hours. She was inconsolable. I was helpless to do anything to ease her pain. With incredible heartache I watched her deal with the pain and told myself I would never put her through anything like that again if I could help it. Sounds like the same song, second verse. I said the same thing about the bladder surgery. A mother only has so much control over a child's life, a hard lesson for me to learn.

Sure enough, the next morning the gap was closed, the pain was gone, and we began the long, arduous task of keeping her teeth clean and the braces clear of food particles. The Water Pik was a lifesaver. She was able to use it independently, and it worked like a charm.

Two years after the rubber bands were applied the braces were removed. What a celebration ensued. Her smile was beautiful, and she had no trouble 'eating the whole thing' from that day forward.

The Bicycle

The summer following her first year at North Broadway School we had gotten Becky an old second hand, fat-tired bicycle hoping that she might learn to ride it. We jogged back and forth, up and down the street, holding on to the seat of the bike while Becky pedaled and guided the bike as well as she could. The route was anything but straight. Day after day her father or I would take her out and go through the routine again and again.

We were not pressuring her. She actually liked riding the bicycle. The summer days flew by, filled with swimming and playing with friends and her kitty cat, Tiger, but the bicycle riding was not getting any better. Becky had begun, sometime during those summer months, to sit on the bike and move it by swinging her legs in wide arcs and pushing off the asphalt with her feet. She became quite efficient at riding in that manner and it seemed to satisfy her.

One day while observing her moving the bike that way, I muttered the following without really expecting any outcome: "Becky, I am so tired of seeing you push that bike with your feet. Why don't you just put your feet on the pedals and ride it like you're supposed to."

"Okay, Mom," she replied, and proceeded to put her feet on the pedals and ride down the street as if she had always done it that way, with perfect balance and riding in a straight line. I let out a scream of surprise and ran into the house to drag her father out. I knew he wouldn't believe it unless he saw it for himself. Sure enough, there she was turning around at the end of the block and *riding back.* We had to help her stop that first time, but with a little instruction on braking, she was off and riding all by herself. It brought back fond memories of her walking, riding her tricycle, singing solos, and the best was yet to come.

In the Swim

I had been a swimming instructor since I was 19 years old. I took life saving and water safety in college with the goal of working outdoors in the summers between school years. In fact, I began dating my first husband and my children's father as a result of teaching swimming and lifeguarding for the YMCA in Colorado Springs in 1960. I taught swimming at CSU and for the City of Boulder in the '60's and 70's. I loved it and was determined that my children would become accomplished swimmers. I didn't learn to swim until I was thirteen years old, and I insisted that my children learn at a much younger age.

My mother and I took Becky and my uncle Harry on a trip to the Four Corners when Becky was a year old. We visited the Sand Dunes, Mesa Verde, and Natural Bridges in Utah. While camping in Mesa Verde, I took Becky into the shower with me. She had only taken baths up to this point and she was terrified of the water coming down on her head. I shut the water off and tried to calm her down. I then remembered how she had balked at going into the Boulder Reservoir with her father a couple of times last summer. The terrified look on her face when she saw that vast expanse of water was hard to erase from my memory.

The children got involved in swimming lessons when we were in Fort Collins, but Becky didn't take to the water at all. When I taught at Scott Carpenter pool in Boulder, the children went with me everyday. Cindy and Todd progressed nicely, but Becky required special attention. Interestingly enough, not one of my children would let me teach them a thing about the water. I turned them over to very competent instructors. I even began bribing the teachers. I offered lunches out, dinner at my house, flowers and candy if only they could get Becky to put her face in the water. The summer she was nine she finally accomplished that feat.

A year later she was at North Broadway School with Barbara, the miracle worker, as her PE teacher. Soon she was able to float, kick, use her arms and even swim a bit. After two or three years she was able to do the front crawl, back crawl, breast stroke and butterfly, but jump into the deep water? Not on your life. The bribery continued until the summer she turned 20. Someone, somewhere, convinced her that she could survive jumping into water over her head. Whew!! It only took 20 years. Lucky for me no one took me up on my offers. I would probably be broke for sure.

Becky waiting for her heat

When Barbara told me Becky was doing the breaststroke and the butterfly in the Special Olympic Swim meet I was incredulous.

"Not possible," I said.

"Oh, yeah?" replied Barb, "just watch."

Becky dived into the water and performed the most coordinated, efficient butterfly you might ever imagine. She showed me again, didn't she? *I* can't even do the butterfly.

A Good Laugh

Becky was always good for a laugh. Her naiveté was so refreshing and her gullibility brought laughter and humor to our lives.

One day when she was about eight or nine years old her father was playing 'chase' with her. He would follow her up and down the stairs, in and out of rooms and eventually she would lock herself in the downstairs bathroom. Her brother and sister would stand outside the door and try to convince her that the coast was clear, that it was all right to come out. "Dad is nowhere in sight," they would exclaim.

"Dad's not out here, Beck. Honest he's not." They would cry trying their best to assure her.

Of course, he was waiting for her, ready to pounce. The squeals of laughter when she finally opened the door to find him waiting there were a delight to hear. It was rare for him to take the time for such 'nonsense', but he was a big tease and she loved it.

They traded places and she became the chaser. Up and down the stairs, in and out of all the rooms they scurried until he locked himself in the downstairs bathroom. She positioned herself strategically outside of the door and then said, "I'm not out here, Dad. Honest I'm not."

We all laughed until we cried.

North Broadway Goes Public

In the spring of 1974 Barbara Shore called me and asked me to attend a meeting at North Broadway School. I was instructed to sit and take notes and pretend that I was one of the instructors. Barb did not want the Director of Special Education to know that I was a parent. I trusted Barb enough to comply with her wishes. At the time I was the President of the Board of Directors for the Sheltered Workshop, which had direct oversight of the school.

It seems that Mr. Baribeau, the Boulder County School District's Special Education Director, was speaking to the teachers about North Broadway School becoming a public school. The school district was poised to take over when school started in the fall. If that happened none of the current teachers would be retained because they lacked the certification required in the public school system. There would be no time to establish a curriculum for the different age groups and ability levels. It did not seem feasible that this plan would serve our children well. To add fuel to the fire, Mr. Baribeau made statements that incited my ire. Statements like: "These parents don't want an education for their children, they just want someone to babysit them." or "We just need to keep them occupied. Let them sit in a corner and finger paint." or "It doesn't matter how long the bus ride is. It won't bother them."

I couldn't take notes fast enough, and it was difficult to camouflage my paper and pencil. I asked for clarification a couple of times because I could not believe what I was hearing. This sacrilege was coming out of the mouth of the Special Education director?

I called an emergency meeting of the Workshop Board and we planned our approach. The husband of one of the school's speech therapists was a graduate student at the University of Colorado studying group dynamics and social interaction. He agreed to organize and facilitate a group of parents, and plans were formulated to attend the School Board meeting where the decision was to be made regarding the school's status.

Each of the participants was given a single point of view to present. We wrote our speeches, practiced them, and adapted them as the group critiqued them. We contacted the school board president to inform him of our plans and were told to make multiple copies of all our information and arguments and have them in the school board members' hands two weeks prior to the meeting. Our work was cut out for us. We compiled the materials and delivered them to the school district well before the meeting.

The School Board met in the school administration building in a room that seated about 150 people. The night of the meeting our supporters filled every seat. The sign on the door might have read 'SRO.' We were prepared to take on the entire school district.

Floyd Baribeau and Ruth Wood, the director of the Boulder County Board for Developmental Disabilities, a program under the auspices of the Colorado Department of Institutions which provided state funded support for the school, entered the room and, to their dismay, saw that the parents, teachers and friends of the North Broadway students filled the auditorium. They excused themselves, entered a small room at the back and emerged about fifteen minutes later. They announced that we had won without even using our ammunition. They would give us two years to get North Broadway School ready for transitioning to the public school system. A curriculum would be developed, and the teachers would be able to gain certification. What a victory!!! Our children would not be thrown to the wolves.

Motorcycle Mania

In 1972 I missed a fly ball during warm-up before a softball game. I wasn't paying attention when it was hit, so my timing was off. I caught it with my face, missing it by a fraction of second. It broke my nose and my jaw and my face swelled up like a puffer fish. I even scared the kids in the waiting room at the doctor's office with my bruised and swollen features. They hid their faces in their mommies' laps.

The day after the crisis my coach, Denny, and his girlfriend, Anita, came by the house to make sure I was all right. By then I had been to the emergency room and been taken care of, but nothing could change the way I looked except time and ice packs. I was a freak and they thought I would always look that way. I had to laugh.

Denny and Anita rode motorcycles. When we walked them out to the street Don walked around Denny's bike and was obviously admiring it. "Do you want to take it around the block?" Denny asked.

"Could I?" asked Don trying to conceal his excitement.

Denny proceeded to show him the ignition, brakes and gears and briefly explained how to ride. Don put on a helmet and took off around the curve at the beginning of our street. It didn't take long for us to realize we could no longer hear the loud putt-putt of the engine. We hurried around the bend and there sat Don at the stop sign sitting patiently on a silent motorcycle. It wasn't even idling. Denny had forgotten to tell him he had to downshift when he came to a stop. With that information, he was off again.

He was sold! Within a week he had purchased a little 2-stroke Suzuki 350 motorcycle. He was elated. It didn't take him long to decide he needed a bigger bike, so he bought himself a Suzuki 550 and I inherited the 350. We both became addicted to motorcycle riding. Besides, it was one way that he would spend time with the family.

Becky on the Kawasaki 1300

That same summer he found a Kawasaki 1300 for sale on a trip to the Canadian Rockies. It was parked in a front yard in a town in Montana. He bought it on the spot with help from the bank and me. I had two hours to run to the Credit Union and borrow money to put in his account. The owner was going to call the bank to make sure his check was good. I still don't know how I was able to pull that off.

The Kawasaki was big enough to hold two kids as passengers and I took the other one on my bike. On weekends we would take short jaunts through the mountains to Estes Park or over the Peak-to-Peak Highway. The kids loved it and so did I.

On one of those short trips Becky was sitting behind her brother on their Dad's bike. I was close enough to see that she was dozing off, rocking from side to side on the back of the motorcycle. I quickly accelerated and pulled up beside Don and motioned for him to pull over. She was so close to falling off; it was heart-stopping for me. From that day forward she had to sit in the middle.

We should have known it might be a problem. Any trip we took in the car put Becky to sleep within a mile of home. Why would a motorcycle have been any different?

Family Pets

SCOOPER
Having read somewhere that kids who are raised with animals are more stable and loving and well rounded, and having wished for a dog my entire childhood, I decided to acquire a puppy for the children. I found a cockapoo-pomeranian puppy in the free ads of the paper and called to put one on hold. She was so tiny I could carry her in my hand throughout the grocery store and no one was the wiser. I probably would have been kicked out of the store had anyone known I was shopping with dog in hand. She was adorable. We named her Scooper after the 'Super Duper Pooper Scooper', a tool for cleaning up after household pets.

Becky with Scooper

Todd was about five years old when we got her. Early one morning I heard the dog yelping downstairs and hurried to see what was happening. It seems she had nipped Todd and he reacted by pushing her away. He did not know that she would tumble down four stairs to the family room floor. She was crying and unable to bear weight on her right front leg. I scooped her up and Becky and I took her to see Dr. Tracy, a local veterinarian who had been highly recommended. He was a gentle soul who loved animals. It was so obvious by the way he handled them and talked to them. He examined Scooper and told me her shoulder was dislocated and he would set it and she would be fine after a couple of weeks. I left her there feeling that she was in the best hands.

He called me later that day to inform me that it was more serious than he'd originally thought and he was going to take her to the veterinary school at Colorado State University. It would have to be pinned and required more expertise than he had. I told him I couldn't afford to pay for such expensive treatment and we might have to put her down. When we got her our agreement was that we would not and could not afford veterinarian charges that exceeded our budget.

"There will be no charge," he replied.

"What are you saying?" I asked.

"After I saw the way your daughter looked at Scooper, there is no way I can put her down. I will cover the fees."

I offered to do whatever I could to help allay the costs; clean his office, make phone calls, do book work, whatever it would take. He just smiled and told me it was his pleasure to help us out. Scooper lived twelve years and was the best watch dog in the world, all seven pounds of her. She yapped and yipped every time the doorbell rang.

TWINKIE

I've already mentioned that Becky loved cats. We tried three times to keep a kitty. The first one got pregnant and ran away. The second was meaner than a junkyard dog and we gave her to a farmer to help keep barn mice under control. The third was Tiger, the cat Becky wouldn't relinquish to the doorframe in an earlier portion of this story. It turned out that Becky broke out in hives every time she held the cat, so he was given to a family down the street who just loved him. In fact, he got lost on one of their trips and someone found him and sent him back to them by air. What dedication!

In 1975 I was the head swimming instructor at South Boulder Recreation Center in Boulder, Colorado. My swim aide was a young man named Dick Rubeck. He **loved** his cat. One night the cat was hit by a car and died and he went into an immediate depression. He didn't come to work that day, but the next day he was inundated with kittens donated by many of us in hopes of assuaging his grief. I was one of those donors. On the way to the pool that day Becky and I stopped at a home to pick up a kitten that had been advertised in the paper, a little calico that was irresistible. Dick had so many kittens to choose from and ours was not his choice. What was I going to do with this little kitty?

Keep it, of course. On the way home we stopped at the store and bought kitty litter and pan, food dish and food and a cat toy. We took it home and set it up in the family room. When the kids' Dad came home he took one look at that cat and motioned to me to come speak with him.

"What is this? A cat? Isn't Scooper enough to take care of?"

"We don't have to keep her," I replied. "I guess I can take her back where I got her."

Ever the people-pleaser, he looked at me and said, "What? You want me to be the bad guy? I guess we can keep her, but I want nothing to do with taking care of her."

We named her Twinkie and she became an integral part of the family. She was really Becky's kitty. If you asked Todd he would tell you that she tormented the cat. She would drag her out from under the bed by her front paws, and Becky sported more cat scratches than anyone I had ever known. Twinkie loved Becky. She would lick her face and purr when Becky finally got her in hand. I read somewhere that cats only lick people they love.

Twinkie warned me one night that Todd's pillow was smoldering on his bed in his basement room. She noodged and noodged (Yiddish meaning to annoy or bother with constant requests, complaints or urging) until I finally got up and followed her down the stairs. She stopped

Becky and her favorite cat Twinkie

abruptly and, playing English pointer, fixed her gaze at the top bunk. Todd fell asleep with his bed lamp still on and it had fallen forward and caused the pillow to smolder.

I yanked him off the bunk and to the floor, grabbed the burning pillow and threw it in the washing machine, the only available source of water in the basement. He was in a daze. I'm sure he couldn't figure out why his mother would treat him in such an irresponsible manner. He soon realized that Twinkie had saved him from serious injury and our house from burning down.

Another time Becky let her out of the car after having been asked to please stay in the car while I purchased meat at the meat market. When Becky walked into the store, I knew the cat had gotten out of the car. We had just taken her to the vet for shots and were on the way home when I decided to stop at the butcher's.

We looked and looked for Twinkie; she was nowhere to be found. The kids' father even jumped into the foray and drove miles looking for the cat. He had become more attached than he cared to admit. We posted reward signs all over the area and went home to wait.

Twenty-four hours later, after no calls, I called the Humane Society. It was early evening and a heavy snow was falling; the forecast was formidable.

"Has a calico cat been found in the last 24 hours?" I asked.

The voice on the other end said, "Why, yes. She was just turned in today."

"Does she have subtle scars on her nose?" was my next question.

After checking her he informed me that she did in fact have scars on her nose.

"That's my cat!" I said. "Don't let anything happen to her. I can't come out in this weather, but I will be there first thing in the morning to pick her up. My children will be so happy."

A woman in the Mapleton Mobile Home Park, some four miles from where she escaped, found her and knew she belonged to someone because she was so healthy and well cared for. She was making her way home, another four miles. Unbelievable!

Becky moved out of our house when Twinkie was about twelve years old. With Becky gone the cat started acting weird. She would sit in the middle of our street, which was really like a narrow lane, and dare the cars to hit her. Some nights I would come home from work and she would be sitting in the middle of my parking place in the garage, almost like hoping I wouldn't notice and would put her out of her misery.

Her demise occurred one evening when Wally, my second husband, pulled into the driveway. As he neared the garage and opened the door, Twinkie emerged from the evergreens by the front stoop and proceeded to walk in front of the car. Wally came to a stop and allowed her to pass unharmed. He then slowly pulled into the garage, and, unbeknownst to him, Twinkie made a U-turn and walked right under the rear wheels. She died instantly.

All we could surmise was that she had a death wish. I think she really missed Becky, in spite of what Todd perceived as Becky's torture and torment of her. She was a very special kitty.

SHADOW

Shadow was born on July 4, 1976, a bi-centennial dog. He was one of nine pedigreed golden retrievers bred by a wealthy family who happened to be good friends of a co-worker. The husband of the couple was climbing Mount Everest and his wife was going as far as the first base camp, so my friend was asked to 'dogsit' the nine puppies. She did so with the agreement that two of the puppies would be given to her.

I had long ago expressed to her that I wanted a big, gentle dog for my children. I felt that Todd, who had already injured Scooper, and Becky, with her inability to handle things gently due to her birth injury, would both benefit from having a large dog that could take the everyday, not-so-often gentle roughhousing of its owners. My friend blessed us with the gift of an adorable 6-week-old golden puppy already named Shadow.

Shadow was the best dog I have ever had the pleasure of knowing. He was so easy to train and so obedient. We had a built-in outdoor grill and he never came near any meat that was left unattended. He would not cross the road until given an 'okay' nod from Wally. He knew his place in the house and never stepped beyond those limits.

Once Wally was part of our lives, he ran with Shadow every day after work. The dog, at no less than ninety pounds, would leap into the air

Becky and Shadow on the deck

and do a 360 degree turn before landing on all fours when he would see Wally walk past the sliding glass door with his running shoes in hand. Shadow never needed a leash. He would answer the call. He never ran away. He was a love.

He died at age twelve of cancer, which is not uncommon in golden retrievers. He just peacefully went to sleep one day in the back yard. He was buried along a favorite running trail by a favorite swimming hole. We have never gotten another pet because we know we could not find another dog as special as Shadow.

A Move to the Suburbs

When Becky was fifteen years old we moved from our comfortable little neighborhood in the city of Boulder to a higher-class neighborhood in the county. Her father had gotten out of the educational field and into real estate and wanted to live in a bigger, more prestigious home. The house was on a narrow, winding street that was the main entrance to the subdivision. We lived across the street from a golf course and about four blocks from a small shopping area.

Our years on Idylwild Trail were sprinkled with the ups of Becky's achieving greater independence and the downs of more trips to the doctor and the hospital. As you might have gathered, Becky is accident prone, not due to lack of attention to her environment as much as her poor balance and gait related to the brain damage. When she was about ten or eleven she fell roller-skating and fractured the humerus in her left arm. We had to cut off her sweatshirt to examine the arm; she was unable to lift it over her head. The doctor made a plaster cap for her elbow and taped the arm close to her body and it healed nicely in a few weeks.

Not long after moving into the house on Idylwild Trail our sewer backed up. The whole basement floor was covered with raw sewage. I had a needle puncture in my thumb from my sewing machine, which became instantly infected once I reached into the nasty, viscous fluid to open the drain. This done before I realized it was sewage. I ran quickly to the store and bought several gallons of Clorox for sterilizing the floor once the muck had drained. We had called the county to blow out the pipes and release the blockage, and I planned to douse the floor with gallons of Clorox to disinfect it.

By the time I got home, Becky had walked ***barefoot*** through the disgusting residue on the floor. I could see her footprints tracked all over the concrete floor. She had gone down the basement to get the cat and traipsed right through the virulent slog.

To make matters worse she had an open wound on the great toe of her left foot, that too, became infected. Once the doctor had examined it, he decided she had osteomyelitis. The bacteria had entered through the open wound and settled in the bones of her great toe. We were informed that if the antibiotics didn't eliminate the infection she could lose her toe. "What next?" I asked myself. It was our good fortune that the toe healed with no significant aftereffects. She has a strong constitution, thank goodness.

Tonsillectomy

Three months later Becky had a positive strep culture three times in four weeks. She would take ten days' worth of antibiotics and within two days have another positive culture. This happened three times running. It was more than I could bear. I looked our pediatrician in the eye and asked, "Do you think we can do a tonsillectomy now?"

Chagrined, he gave me a half-smile and reluctantly said, "Yes, mother, I think it would be best."

The surgery was scheduled with the ear, nose and throat doctor about a month hence. In the meantime I had been to see my OB-Gyn for an annual checkup and had whined about the futility of wanting to have Becky's tubes tied or a hysterectomy performed to prevent an unwanted pregnancy. Having lived with her for sixteen years, I was well aware that she would not be able to carry, bear, or raise a child on her own. I knew in my heart it would be most difficult to abort my grandchild. He consoled me and assured me that he would be able to perform that surgery while she was having her tonsils removed. I shook my head slowly, took a deep breath, and informed him that it would not be possible.

The state legislature had passed a law that proclaimed a developmentally disabled person could not be sterilized without that person's permission. The process of gaining her understanding of the situation and giving her permission would take about two years, and she might not ever be able to or want to agree to such a procedure. He looked at me with disbelief and said, "I don't believe you! That's criminal. Not only should she not have to worry about getting pregnant, but she shouldn't have to deal with menstruation every month."

I assured him that I knew what I was talking about, having kept myself apprised of any and all legislation that involved disabled people. He insisted on checking with his lawyer before giving up on the idea.

He called me three days later and said, "Holly, you were exactly right. I can't touch her with a ten foot pole!"

The tonsillectomy went like clockwork, and Becky soon recovered; she loved eating ice cream and popsicles, pudding and Jell-O. Soon she was back to her usual level of activity. She has had strep but a few times since her tonsils were removed.

One of those times was at the Easter Seal Camp in Eagle County. The counselors called me to come pick her up. They originally thought she had the flu, but when I heard the symptoms I knew it was strep. She gets a high fever and her equilibrium is all out of whack. Penicillin took care of it right away.

Another time she developed those symptoms while residing at the Manhattan Apartments. The counselor called and wanted me to okay a CT scan because her balance was so badly affected they were concerned about a brain disorder. Once they described the symptoms to me, I assured them it was strep and required neither a scan nor charging Medicaid an exorbitant amount for an unnecessary test. It *was* strep and I asked if they would please note on the front of her personal file the symptoms she displays when strep has infected her body. A simple solution, don't you think? Communication is the bottom line.

Another Broken Bone?

One day a year or so later she asked if she could go for a bike ride. I reminded her to watch for cars when she entered the street, and off she went. It was very hard for me to let her go alone. I forced myself to continue with what I was doing rather than watch to make sure she was riding safely. I must have become immersed in my activity, because I was unaware that she had returned home and quietly crawled into bed.

A bit later I became concerned because, to my knowledge, she had not returned. I went outside to look for her, and, when she was nowhere in sight, became concerned. After traversing on foot all the paths and roads nearby, I was becoming anxious. I decided I needed to get in the car and drive through the neighborhood to look for her. I passed her bedroom on the way to retrieve my car keys, and there she was, sound asleep in her bed. Relieved, I wakened her only to note that her right hand was scraped and swollen to twice its normal size. Doggedly, I questioned her about what happened. She just shrugged her shoulders and answered, "I don't know." She was not able to tell me where or when or how it happened; we just knew it happened on her bike ride.

As I looked at the hand, I decided it might be broken, so off to the emergency room we went. We were admitted and waited for an ER doctor to retrieve us. When he finally called our name, he took one look at Becky and asked her what happened. You guessed it. Her response was "I don't know." Nor could I give him any specifics.

After examining her hand, he looked at me, and with total seriousness said, "I think it's just an infection. I'll prescribe some antibiotics, and it should improve in a few days."

He thought he was going to get away with that. I narrowed my eyes and told him "I want it X-rayed."

He was not in the least bit happy with me, and had no choice but to take her to X-ray. Sheepishly, he walked out later with the finished X-ray in hand and said, "I guess you were right, mother. It's broken."

So, again, Becky had a plaster accessory. This one taped to her fractured hand.

Summer School

The summer of 1977 Becky's school initiated a summer program and, because I was working at the South Boulder Recreation Center, she was registered to participate. With her in a summer program, I didn't need to worry about finding someone to stay with her while I was working.

Becky

The issue then became how to get her home from the program. North Broadway School was at the opposite end of town from the recreation center. We decided she could take the city bus that stopped right in front of her school and could drop her off at the rec center. This was a big step toward independence for Becky.

We took a trial run so she would know where to get on and off the bus and how much money to put in the receptacle. She seemed very confident that she could do this by herself. As I dropped her off at school the first day, I asked her to show me how much money it would take to ride the bus. She was visibly upset and told me, in no uncertain terms, that she knew what a dime and nickel were and off she went.

I was waiting at the other end of the bus route when she got off four hours later, all smiles and self-assured. Her look told me, "See, Mom, I did it all by myself."

Thus began our routine. It went without a hitch until the day that she didn't get off the bus. No Becky!!

I ran to my car and sped off after the bus. I followed it all the way into downtown Boulder where it had a short layover. I parked the car and sprinted to the idle bus, bounded up the steps and, gasping for breath, asked the driver if he'd picked up my daughter at North Broadway School. Before he could answer I began describing her to him while I scanned the seats of the bus. The poor man didn't have a chance to respond as I noticed Becky's feet splayed out into the aisle. In three giant steps I was beside her as she slept soundly. With a great sigh of relief I wakened her. She looked at her surroundings and me, and I'm sure had no idea what I was doing on the bus. I was overjoyed to see her, gave her a hug, and we got off the bus.

Another time she did not arrive as scheduled, and it was not possible for me to follow the bus. I called the dispatcher at the Regional Transportation District (RTD) and told her my dilemma. I was much calmer knowing that Becky had probably fallen asleep again. The dispatcher assured me that she would follow up and call back when they located her. Before she could call me, the route supervisor intercepted the bus, retrieved Becky, and brought her to the recreation center. I was overwhelmed with gratitude for his concern and actions. There are good people in this world.

Bobby

Bobby was Becky's 'boyfriend'. Their first encounter was at age 6 at Washington School in Mrs. Woodrum's class, and they were classmates at North Broadway School. Having a boyfriend for Becky was just that, a friend who was a boy. Bobby was a young man who looked normal and on first impression seemed normal. His IQ was somewhere in the 70-80 range. One realized that he had some disability when he repeatedly asked, "So how're ya doin?" He had a difficult home life, but was pleasant enough most of the time.

Becky and Bobby

He, too, attended summer school that year, and the school group came to South Boulder Rec Center to use the paddleboats on Viele Lake, one of the summer activities offered by the rec department. I was teaching swimming and came upstairs to speak to the front desk person. I noticed Bobby pacing back and forth and muttering to himself.

I approached him and asked, "What's going on, Bobby? Is everything all right?"

He responded, "That God-damned Becky! She won't ride in the paddleboat with me. She'd rather ride with Lane. I'm going to kick her in the balls."

I entertained the notion of trying to explain to him how that was not possible but instead chose to try to calm him down and encourage him to find another partner. They remained friends into their late 20's, and then his behavior became so bizarre I discouraged the relationship.

Prom

In 1979 North Broadway School decided the older students should have a prom, complete with dinner and dancing, corsages and boutonnieres.

Lane asked Becky to be his date and she accepted. She wore a long skirt and looked quite ladylike. His mother drove them to the Broker Restaurant where they met the rest of the schoolmates. The school secretary, Doreen, had agreed to be the chaperone. The students all loved her and she returned that love.

The Broker Restaurant's usual fare included a huge shrimp bowl as an appetizer. Most of the young people at the table had never had shrimp before and were eating them whole. Doreen didn't realize it until one of them complained about having difficulty chewing the tails. Stifling her laughter, she then demonstrated the correct way to eat shrimp. It was much more enjoyable for the diners after those instructions.

When their 'drinks' were delivered, Doreen suggested they have a toast. Becky looked at her and blurted out, "Doreen, toast is what you have for breakfast."

The joy of time spent with those whose egos are not in play, who don't care about status and appearances, is priceless. The majority of those prom attendees had never been to a fancy restaurant. What an experience that must have been for them!

A Walk to the Store

That same year I was studying for my orals. I had undertaken a Master's program in 1977 and was hoping to graduate in June. I was inundated with books and notes and other study materials when Becky asked me if she could go to King Soopers, our local grocery store. It was about six blocks away. I hated telling her that I couldn't take her because I really had to study. I suggested maybe we could do it another day.

"I can go by myself," she said confidently.

I stopped what I was doing and gave that some deep thought. Talking to myself I thought, "Okay, smarty, you're the one who's always telling other parents to let their kids go. You're the one who's constantly encouraging independence. Time to put your words into action."

I gave her permission to walk to the store but encouraged her to cross the golf course and avoid Lookout Road, a busy through street that bordered our subdivision on the north. She said "Okay" and bounded out the door. I buried myself in my books and papers and time passed. Suddenly I realized that she had been gone longer than expected. I asked her brother, Todd, to go look for her. No sooner had he started for the door than she walked in through the garage.

"Becky, where have you been so long? Did you cross the golf course like I asked you to do?"

"No, Mom. I used the street. There were too many golfers."

So there! Who can't make wise decisions? I often ask myself what mentally challenged really means.

Becky made walking to the store with our golden retriever Shadow part of her daily routine. All the storeowners along her route got to know her and looked forward to her regular jaunts to the shopping area.

After she moved out of the house, they let me know how much they missed seeing her. She made lasting impressions everywhere she went.

A Not So Wise Decision

Becky was a collector. She collected freebies, i.e. bus schedules, advertising pamphlets, newspapers and magazines that were there for the taking in the lobby of the grocery store with titles such as "Where to Live in Boulder," "Where to Dine in Boulder,' "Things to do in Boulder," and real estate come-ons. She would fill her backpack with them and bring them home and fill her drawers. She didn't do anything with them; she just liked having them in her possession.

It's a little hard for people with developmental disabilities to separate or understand that some things are free and others have prices attached. On her daily jaunts to the super market she would help herself to the freebies and then wander through the store. She had money to spend, but didn't think she had to pay for magazines. They looked just like the things in the entryway so they must be there for the taking. She added <u>Cosmopolitan,</u> complete with a Bert Reynolds centerfold, <u>Vogue,</u> and <u>Woman's Day</u> to her stash in her backpack and walked out the door.

One of the sackers, a woman named Elaine, observed her shoplifting and tried to stop her. Becky is very strong and fortunately doesn't know how strong she is. Her backpack is her most prized possession. Nobody touches it, and no one can get permission to touch it. Becky pushed Elaine away and kept walking. Another clerk, a man named Stan, ran to Elaine's side and assured her that she should let Becky go. He knew us and would call and have us handle it from home. The phone call was a most unwelcome one.

When Becky walked in the door I confronted her. I asked to look in her backpack, and she adamantly refused. I then, without thinking, tried to take it from her and she fought like a cornered tiger. I managed to take it away from her. I think the only reason I was able to overcome her was because I was her mother. Tearfully she admitted to taking the magazines. I explained to her the difference between the free materials in the front of the store and the magazines on the shelves. She let me remove them, and we decided she would return them and apologize.

I called the store and asked to speak to the manager. I informed him that we were on our way and asked if he would please let her know that she could be arrested for shoplifting and put in jail.

"Oh, I don't think I can do that," he said.

"I am asking you to do that. She needs to know that what she did is not okay and that there are consequences."

He played the role to a tee. She was obviously shaken and promised not to ever do it again. She didn't until a few years later when a room-mate aided and abetted her.

Hawaii

Grandpa Meyers passed away in 1978. He'd been fighting Hodgkin's disease for two years and finally succumbed. A year later Grandma Meyers was re-marrying a gentleman named Bill whose wife had also died of cancer. The wedding was in the spring of 1980 in San Mateo, California and was to be followed by a honeymoon in Hawaii. The whole family was invited to go along, the five of us, Don's sister, hus-band and two kids, Bill's former brother-in-law and wife and his older brother and spouse. The entire event was a fiasco from beginning to finish in my estimation. (I guess it could have been because they were my *in-laws*.)

Grandma Meyers told us, in no uncertain terms, that our children "were not to wear tennis shoes to her wedding!" We outfitted Todd in slacks, dress shirt and shiny shoes and the girls wore their prom dresses. All the finery was packed and checked at the airport. The airlines sent it through to Hawaii, and there we sat in the San Francisco Airport with no luggage. By some stroke of good fortune we got it back the next morn-ing, six hours before 'the wedding' was to take place. Thank goodness! None of us wanted to endure Grandma's wrath.

Becky

We arrived in Honolulu late the next morning and had to walk or ride six to eight blocks to a smaller airport to catch a Hawaiian hop to Kauai. In pouring rain thirteen of us walked the six blocks to the airport, lugging our baggage and herding kids. The groom's brother, Fred, and wife, in their 80's, were offered a ride by an airport employee with a golf cart.

They didn't arrive at the airport and, after we missed two planes, it was decided that the women and children should go ahead and Bill and Don would go look for the missing couple. It seems the airport employee could only take them within the perimeter of the airport's property, and they were dropped off on a corner in the tropical downpour. There they stood, soaking wet, waiting for someone to rescue them. Fred had been told as a child, were he ever lost, to stay in one place and be visible. It worked. Two hours later we were all together in Kauai.

We spent three days in Kauai and then boarded a plane for Maui. We checked into a luxury hotel on Kaanapali Beach and the kids couldn't wait to go into the water. Between pulling the three-year-old son of Don's sister out of the waves and voluntarily supervising the beachfront, I was not the most pleasant person to be around. I simply wanted to be left alone to read a book in peace and quiet.

Out of nowhere Becky walked up behind me and said, "Mom, I got my thing."

"What do you mean, you got your 'thing?' I countered.

"You know. My Thing."

Then it struck me. The girls at Becky's school called their menstrual period their 'thing'. Mind you she was eighteen years old. I had almost decided she would never menstruate. There we were in Hawaii, on the beach, and Becky had her first period.

I jumped up, brushed the sand off my body, grabbed my towel and proceeded to the hotel's convenience store, hand in hand with Becky. We bought sanitary napkins and a belt and, returning to the privacy of our room, had a lesson on the art of applying Kotex.

I returned to the beach and the sand and my book and within a couple of hours Becky was back telling me she needed more pads. She must have been so excited she changed it every ten minutes whether she needed to or not. Now my special little girl was a woman, at least in body if not in spirit.

Special Olympics

Becky started participating in Special Olympics when she was ten years old. Her first events were sprints and long jump. Later on rumor had it that she won the long jump even though she sat down because her legs were so long. She competed every year and brought home ribbons by the yard.

Becky running the 50 yard dash

After she learned to swim she competed in aquatic events. She swam the front crawl, backstroke, and breaststroke competitively. Standing six feet tall and with very long arms, she seemed a natural. Interestingly enough, she would finish a heat and then burst into tears. We were never able to figure out what the tears were about. Was it relief? Anxiety? Excitement?

I served on the state board for Special Olympics, and, because I had been a swim instructor for most of my adult life, I was put in charge of the swimming program for the state. In those days the meet was held at the Air Force Academy. The freshman class was required to stay an extra week after the school year ended in order to help with the Special Olympics. What a perfect venue for the athletes! They were in awe of the surroundings and the 'blue cadets'.

Becky was swimming the backstroke and turned over on her front to touch the wall. I had to disqualify her. It is imperative that backstrokers stay on their backs until they touch. The young cadets working as officials at the swim meet were appalled that I would disqualify anyone. I informed them that she was my daughter, and I couldn't play favorites. They continued to harangue about my decision until I said, "These athletes need to learn to play by the rules just like any athlete. Life is not going to let them off the hook, so they might as well learn now about following rules and the consequences of breaking them." I think they had a new respect for me after that incident.

Brockport, New York

The International Special Olympics was in Brockport, New York, in 1979. My mother and I decided to take all three children to New York for the event. Becky was not selected as a contender, but we decided it would be a memorable experience for all of us. On the flight Becky refused to eat anything, unusual for her.

We arrived in Brockport and checked into our hotel. One of my dearest friends lived in Pittsford, just a few miles away. She invited us to come to her house for dinner that first night. Becky was not hungry. She wouldn't even eat a snack. She just sat in a big beanbag chair and showed no interest in anything; she was lethargic.

The next morning she was burning up with fever. Before we did anything else we took her to the emergency room at the local hospital. They checked her out, did a spontaneous strep test and ruled out any infection. We were told it would pass; give her fluids and encourage rest. We returned to the hotel and spent that day in our room.

The next morning she seemed better so we all piled in our rental car and headed for the games. It was drizzling the whole time we were out that day. That night she was no better, so we decided to just play it by ear on a daily basis. Every time she perked up a bit we dragged her out to dinner or to the stadium, thinking it was something that would pass.

After the closing ceremony we decided to visit Niagara Falls. Why not? We were so close how could we pass up the opportunity? Without any further discussion we were off to the Falls. They are huge! Pictures do them no justice. Todd and Cindy, Becky's siblings, wanted to take a boat ride around the falls; with tears in her eyes Becky refused to get in the boat. I think she was fearful of the water, the noise and the idea of being in a boat in the middle of it all. Cindy and Todd thought Becky was faking her illness and didn't hesitate to call her names, like 'sissy' and 'baby'. My mother and the other two children took the boat ride. It must have been a thrill for them to be right next to Niagara Falls. When they disembarked, we decided to take the walk behind the Falls.

We had to put on galoshes and heavy black-hooded Macintoshes. We cajoled Becky into going with us. Little did we know what to expect. The noise was deafening, millions of gallons of water falling every second over the rock wall. Water, water, everywhere. We couldn't hear ourselves think. Becky was miserable. Her fear of water played into her misery and the noise drove her crazy. We exited as quickly as possible, and I was consumed with guilt.

We drove back to Brockport along the shoreline of Lake Ontario. My kids didn't believe we were in New York. Like most kids their age, with their limited travel experience, they thought New York meant New York City. Upstate New York is absolutely beautiful, rolling farmland and open space, nothing like New York City.

When we got home Becky got worse and developed a really deep, hacking cough. It hit me like a ton of bricks that she might have pneumonia. I called our pediatrician, one of those rare doctors who will actually listen to a mother, and he agreed to see her right away. He examined her thoroughly and said, "You're right, Mother. She has pneumonia." The guilt I felt at Niagara Falls didn't begin to compare with the guilt that overwhelmed me at that moment. Becky's brother and sister also experienced a level of guilt when I told them how sick she really was.

She came through that ordeal with her usual flying colors and has had pneumonia twice as an adult. I will never forget how we took her out into that cold, drizzly weather and made her participate in what we wanted to do. Were we selfish and unfeeling? I would say so.

Baptism

DeeDee and Glenn were our next door neighbors on Idylwild Trail. Glenn was the pastor at the local Lutheran Church and DeeDee worked for the Rocky Mountain Synod of the ELCA, Evangelican Lutheran Church of America. She was a very classy lady who dressed to the nines for work every day. Her hair was coiffed to perfection; not a strand out of place. I decided in my finite way that we could probably never be friends. I was a sweatshirt and tennis shoe kind of woman who loved to get down and dirty in the garden. I didn't perceive that I was her type at all.

We existed in our homes side by side with some interaction, but not truly friendship. That is, until that day in the fall of 1983 when Glenn asked if I would speak to the adult Sunday school class at his church on the topic of parenting a child with developmental disabilities. Having done just that for several years at Colorado University for Dr. Happy Martin's abnormal psychology class, I was more than happy to speak at the church.

To give a little background on my church affiliations, I was an agnostic who was totally turned off by the blatant hypocrisy observed in church congregations. I didn't like pushy proselytizers at my door like the Jehovah's Witnesses or the Church of Latter Day Saints, and I thought I had too much to do to get involved in church activities. Our family was unchurched.

Never having attended a Lutheran Church before, I didn't know what to expect. I thought I'd do my presentation and that would be the end of it. I went armed with arguments about why I wasn't interested in attending church. I never had to use them. The people in that church were so gracious and unpretentious and non-aggressive. Not one asked me about joining or my faith or lack thereof. I began attending on a regular basis and took Becky with me when I went.

There were no classes for her, so they let her volunteer as a nursery attendant. Some parents were surprised to see her there and stared as if she were some sideshow freak. They sidled past her as if she had some contagious disease. Others who were more open-minded and accepting, as the Bible says they should be, didn't hesitate to leave their children with Becky in the room. In fact, there were a few kids who would only stop crying when they were in Becky's care. My sense was that she taught a few people a lesson about the phrase, "All God's Children."

After attending Shepherd of the Hills Lutheran Church for a year, Becky agreed to be baptized. You see my children had not been baptized as babies. My theory was that they should be able to choose whether or not they wanted to participate in that rite. Since we didn't attend church during their childhoods, they had no exposure to church traditions and customs.

We began the process for Becky's baptism. She was required to memorize some ritual phrases. Glenn gave me permission to have her repeat them after me. As with the Brownie pledge, we practiced at home until she could repeat all the necessary liturgy. The big day came and, again, she surprised us all by repeating all the baptismal vows from memory. She never tired of putting to rest all the stereotypes afforded to people with disabilities.

Becky and Annie

DeeDee and Glenn had a baby girl a few years after we moved in. They named her Annie. Their philosophy of parenting included teaching her to use the correct names for all the parts of the human body. They weren't going to tolerate any nicknames for male or female genitalia or any other body parts.

Becky and Annie

As Annie grew a bit older she and Becky became buddies. They spent a lot of time together playing with their dolls and just being silly. If Annie wasn't at our house, Becky was at hers. They made quite a picture; Becky at 18 years of age and Annie at three. The ideal Mutt and Jeff. What a pair!

One very warm summer day they asked if they could run through the hose. I hand picked a sprinkler with the broadest, highest spray, attached it to the hose and turned the water on full force. Dressed in their bathing suits they ran through it, squealing with glee as the cool water showered their bodies.

I was at the kitchen sink watching through the window as I washed dishes. All of a sudden I heard Annie shout, "Look, Becky. It's going up my vagina!!"

She was squatting over the sprinkler letting the water drench her little bottom and giggling with joyful little girl sounds. All she needed was a bullhorn so the whole neighborhood could hear. It was delightful to hear a three-year-old use the correct terminology for her anatomy. Becky just laughed, and I'm sure the whole incident went over her head. The fun they had was so innocent and their friendship so ingenuous. Too bad they had to grow up.

Becky as 'Cheer' Leader

Becky's father worked for a real estate company after leaving education and coaching behind. He worked for a company called Court Square Realty, which was an umbrella company that included construction, real estate sales and investments. His immediate supervisor was a gentleman named John. John lived in our subdivision and had to pass our house on his way to and from the office. Soon after we moved, John stopped by for some reason and met Becky for the first time.

He looked at me and asked, "What did you and Don ever do to deserve that?"

I was incredulous. How could he have the gall to ask me that and especially with Becky standing right there? It took all my fortitude to keep from showing him the door and telling him not to darken it again.

Over time and after spending more time in Becky's presence, he must have realized what a gift she had. As I've mentioned before, she smiles all the time and loves life. She has a positive way about her that wins people over if they can just get past their initial curiosity, fear and wonderment. So many people have pre-conceived notions about people who are developmentally disabled.

A few months later he stopped by on his way home from work after a particularly difficult day and said, "You know, sometimes I just have to stop by your house, 'cause Becky always cheers me up." Will wonders never cease?

Dr. Happy Martin

I was accepted at the University of Colorado in 1957 having graduated 15th in a class of 555. I was no dummy. However, I was anything but sophisticated and certainly not an abstract thinker. With my excellent high school GPA, I was eligible for 'honors' classes and assigned to the 'honors' department's dean for scheduling and selection of classes. He suggested I take Intro to Psychology, a sophomore course. I had no clue what I was getting into. I studied like mad for my first midterm and flunked it flat!! I was dragged before the sorority's scholarship board where they demanded to know why I failed. All I could tell them was that I thought I had done well.

I studied my tail off for the second midterm, thought I aced it and again got an 'F.' I was mortified and finally swallowed my pride and went to talk to the professor, Dr. Happy Martin. She was a gentle older woman who told me my grade would depend on how well I did on the final exam. I got a 'C', which averaged out to a 'D' in the course. I also got a 'D' second semester in a sophomore humanities course that was way over my head. I decided at that point to become my own advisor and, if I couldn't do better, would give up my scholarships so someone more capable could take advantage of a college education. For the next three years, I was on the honor roll.

Dr. Martin also taught Abnormal Psychology, and her students were assigned to groups with topics to be presented in any fashion they chose. Somehow they got my name and called me to request my services as a speaker. They wanted me to discuss with the class my experience parenting a 'retarded' child (long before developmentally disabled became the politically correct term). I was more than happy to do that and must have done an acceptable job because my name was passed down semester after semester for the next several years.

One year in the early 80's the group insisted on interviewing me before asking me to present. They came to my house and listened to a synopsis of my story. At one point a student looked me in the eye and asked, "Have you ever let those doctors know that Becky is retarded and why?"

That was food for thought. I had not considered that notion but took her suggestion to heart and began to track Drs. Kerr and Blake. I found Dr. Kerr retired in Arizona someplace. I introduced myself and then launched into a tirade about my daughter and her disabilities and how avoidable they could have been had he just been a little more patient and compassionate.

He stumbled over his words as he tried to explain that he had nothing to do with her disabilities. I let him squirm for several minutes as he tried to cover his actions with his lies and exaggerations and then gently informed that I had no intention of suing him. I just wanted him to know what had happened. His conscience could be his judge and jury.

One of the last years I was invited to speak I introduced myself to Dr. Martin and explained that I had been a student in 1957. I told her how chagrined I was when I received a 'D' the first semester in her class. She looked at me and smiled and said, "Well, my dear, you have earned an 'A' as far as I'm concerned."

I filled with pride and thanked her from the bottom of my heart.

Divorce

I divorced Becky's father in June 1982. We had simply grown apart; had different values; and really had nothing in common. Coming from a family of divorce, my intention was to stay married for the rest of my life. Sometimes things are out of our realm of control. I tried for 22 years to make a go of it, and it just wasn't meant to last.

Becky was 21 years old when we went our separate ways. Her Dad was always very busy and didn't spend much time with the children. He had jobs that kept him away from home and when he was home he focused on other things.

Cindy was eighteen and Todd was fifteen. Don moved out, and they didn't hear much from him. Becky, on the other hand, was in his face, so to speak. She called him often, and every Sunday he took her out to breakfast at McDonald's. She was not going to let him slide. He took her out to breakfast every Sunday for probably 20 years. As she became more and more independent, the breakfasts out became less and less important. Gradually they ended as a regular occasion.

Don divorced his second wife in 2006 and retired a few years after that. Once his workload ended he had time to be a father. This time it was Todd who wouldn't let him off the hook. Todd would take his son, Wiley, over to his Dad's condo and tell him they were there to watch football with him. As time went on Don became immersed in the kids' lives. He babysits the children, 'dogsits' their animals, picks Becky up for family doings, has family gatherings at his condo for July 4th, Memorial Day and Christmas Eve. He is now very much a part of their lives, and it is good to see.

Becky adores her father, and he, as am I, is blessed with a daily phone call from her.

Graduation from Ruth M. Wood School/Burke School

After the transition to the public school system, North Broadway School was re-named The Ruth M. Wood School for the lady who had founded the original school and workshop. After it became a public school things did change for the better. There were more opportunities for the students to be involved in extra-curricular activities and athletics. With the school district footing the bill, there were more opportunities for field trips and excursions into the community. In 1982 the school moved into the vacant Burke Junior High School building and became the Burke School.

Becky went to school until she was 22 years old as the law allowed. During the twelve years she was at Ruth M. Wood School/North Broadway School/Burke she learned to swim, ran track and field, did flips on the trampoline landing on her bottom (but still a flip), sang in the choir, learned independent living techniques and activities of daily living. The teachers did such a marvelous job of preparing her for independence that, when the time came for her to leave home and live elsewhere, she welcomed the opportunity with gleeful acceptance.

She blossomed with the environment that the school offered: teachers who cared deeply about the welfare of their students, administrators who had only the students' best interests at heart, and a staff who wanted each student to reach the apex of his/her abilities.

The school's cook, a woman named Louise, loved each and every student without condition. She started a cooking class in the cafeteria kitchen, rotating the older students through the program on a regular basis until they all could cook something safely and well. I can't name many people in this world who would have had enough patience and love to perform that task. Louise came up with the concept for a restaurant in the school's cafeteria. They called it something like 'The North Broadway Café.' She trained the students to set up, wait tables and buss along with prep work and simple cooking in the kitchen. The school was located in a county building that housed mental health facilities, social services and the workshop. The Café was a godsend for the people who worked in that facility. It was a benefit for them and an even greater benefit for the students. A win/win situation for sure.

Becky graduated from Burke School in June 1983. The graduation ceremony was held in the school's gymnasium complete with 'Pomp and Circumstance' and fancy clothes. Seven students graduated that year. The Burke Bulletin, the school's newspaper, had a graduation edition in which each of the graduates was pictured and a personal interview was printed.

Becky's read as follows:

"Becky says she can hardly wait to graduate because it will be "fun"! She lives with her mom and her brother Todd, but hopes to move to Kellwood House sometime in the future. Her favorite part of school has been P.E. Football is her favorite. She has been a Special Olympian in the past and has participated in many different Olympic activities. This year she went to the State Meet in Colorado Springs as a swimming contestant. She has

Graduation bulletin 1983

been active in the City of Boulder Recreational programs and has taken cooking, swimming and bowling.

She has been on a work-study program this spring and has been employed by the Humane Society doing maintenance work. She loves caring for the small animals there. She has been active at school in singers and hand bell choir and is currently enjoying working with the Apple II computer.

Becky says she will miss her teachers and all her friends here at school. After she graduates, she is hopeful about finding custodial work in the community and has high hopes for her future."

She was dressed in a long cotton gown and fancy shoes; the whole graduation bit. It was a celebration full of smiles until one of her classmates started to cry. That was all it took to trigger tears from Becky. She sat with her legs parted and her head hung between her knees, sobbing loudly and moving from exuberance to nostalgia in mere minutes. So much for dressing her up and expecting her to act like a lady. Diploma in hand she was ready to move on. Independence suited her well. Read on.

Reading

Speaking of reading, Becky never learned to read. There was some disconnect in her brain. Her teachers worked and worked on reading, but all she could ever achieve was recognizing important words, words that she would need to know in order to function as an independent young lady.

A wonderful volunteer at the East branch of the Boulder Public Library near our home offered to work with her one-on-one, tutoring her in reading. After three years she decided it was a lost cause. Becky just didn't have the right wiring for accomplishing that skill.

She was able to recognize the buses she eventually learned to ride. She knew her name and 'Mom' and 'Dad' and 'love' and, most importantly, she could recognize 'Men' and 'Women'. She could be trusted to pick the right door when looking for bathrooms in a public place.

Once, when visiting relatives in Lakewood, Colorado we decided to have lunch at a McDonald's Restaurant. As usual, Becky had to use the bathroom. I pointed her in the right direction and continued conversing with others at the table. A few minutes later I realized she had been gone longer than usual and proceeded to head toward the bathrooms to check on her. Just as I got there she came bopping out of the door marked 'Cowboys' with her usual big grin, so proud that she had done it all independently. Who would have expected the doors to be labeled 'Cowgirls' and 'Cowboys'? Only in the wild West!!

Re-marriage

In August 1984 I remarried. My new husband is Wally von Helms. We met while both of us were working at Boulder Memorial Hospital.

He was a master electrician and had been hired to wire a remodeling job on the second floor. We met quite by accident. He noticed me walking through the halls of the hospital, guitar in hand on my way to Pediatrics. He often asked if I knew "Ragtime Cowboy Joe." Every time he asked I would give him the same 'no' answer, but it didn't deter him.

Over time and weeks of flirting with each other, we finally went out for a drink after work and the rest is history. We had a small wedding at Mount Calvary Lutheran Church with family and close friends in attendance. The reception was held at our home. Flowers from my garden adorned the altar and I prepared all the food for the reception. Friends pitched in to help, and it was a day very worth remembering. The simplicity of the whole affair made it that much more meaningful.

It was a challenge getting Becky to wear something feminine to the wedding. She finally decided on a skirt and blouse and looked quite nice. She and Wally spend a lot time teasing each other, but also have a great deal of respect for one another. He has been willing to provide transportation for her on more than one occasion, and even took her fishing when we still lived in Boulder. He will never replace her father, but he is a positive figure in her life.

Latent Teenager

1984 was a year for change. It had become apparent that Becky was ready to move out of the house and get on with her life. She was working at McDonald's at the time and rode the bus to and from work. She would eat breakfast, get dressed in her uniform and storm out the front door, never saying good-by, kiss my you-know-what or anything. She'd just leave.

One day I simply asked her is she would please let me know when she was leaving. She looked at me as if I were asking her to cut off her hand or something drastic like that. There was no change in her behavior.

One afternoon she didn't get home at the usual time. The minutes turned into a half hour and then began to approach an hour. I finally decided to call the Sheriff and report that something was amiss. I no sooner picked up the phone than she came bounding through the front door.

"Where have you been?" I demanded to know. She looked at me and said, "I stopped at the church to see the bunnies."

It seems the church pre-school had rabbit hutches out in the play yard and Becky wanted to check them out. No concern whatsoever with the fact that her mother was worried beyond worry about her. I asked her then if she thought she might be ready to move to one of the homes sponsored by the Boulder County Board for Developmental Disabilities (BCBDD). She didn't hesitate to say, "Hey, yeah!"

I didn't need a latent teenager giving me heart palpitations. Her brother and sister had put me through hoops and I truly thought I wouldn't go through any teenage rebellion with Becky. She was 23 years old and giving me fits like a 16 year old. It was time.

Moving Out

I began the discussion process with the counselors at the BCBDD, and it was decided that she should spend a weekend at Kelwood House, a group home on the hill near Colorado University. They would be able to evaluate her in the living situation and make a recommendation for placement.

The residential program was based on abilities and worked on a graduated scale, so to speak. Those who needed the most supervision moved into Carmel house first. Carmel House had three floors. The residents moved into the first floor upon acceptance and subsequently moved to the upper floors according to their progress in independent living. When they reached the goals required to move out, they could go to Kellwood House or Iris Place. From those residences the next step was the Manhattan Apartments, named so because it was located on Manhattan Place.

Manhattan consisted of four apartments in a bi-level building. Each apartment housed two residents who shared meal preparation and dining with their neighbors on the same floor. A live-in counselor supervised their living situations, made doctors' appointments, took them grocery shopping, assured that they left for work on time. It was a big step up from Kellwood.

Becky passed the test at Kellwood House with flying colors and they put her on the waiting list. The decision had been made; we just had to wait for an opening.

At that time I worked as a recreation therapist at Boulder Memorial Hospital's Rehab Unit. I started working there in April 1981. I worked a four-day week, ten hours a day so I didn't get home until after 7:00 p.m. Becky often was alone at home from the time she got home from school and later home from work. She was very responsible and I had no reason to worry about her.

One Friday night, as I was teaching my evening water aerobics class in the therapy pool, lightning lit up the mountain outside of the pool. The thunderclaps were so close that I called off the class and sent everyone home. I drove home in a pounding cloudburst, the rain falling so hard that visibility was nearly zero.

I pulled into the driveway and, as the garage door was opening noticed someone in my yard with a shovel in hand. It was my neighbor, Gary, digging a ditch to pull the water away from the house.

I hurried into the house and found Becky and DeeDee, the pastor's wife who had become a close friend, in the basement. DeeDee was frantically sweeping the water that was pouring through the window wells toward the drain. It looked like a minor version of Niagara Falls.

I shouted at DeeDee, "What are you doing here?"

"Becky called and said she had a 'mergency!", she answered.

Becky not only called DeeDee she called Gary also, and they came running to help. Our house was built on bentonite clay and shifted constantly depending on the weather. We often had water in the basement but never as much as there was that night.

I was amazed. She did exactly what any 'normal' person should have done in that situation. She knew she needed help and she acted. What a kid!

The next day I called Kellwood House and the residential counselor at the BCBDD and informed them of Becky's actions. I inserted my opinion that she was ready for Manhattan Place. If she could keep her wits about her and was sensible enough to call for help in my absence, why couldn't she live in the Manhattan Apartments?

They agreed and put her on the waiting list for Manhattan. They said it might be a couple of years before a room would be available, so we hunkered down and decided to survive until such a time. Three months later I received a call at the hospital informing me that there was a room for Becky at Manhattan. It seems the girl who most recently occupied that room had psychological problems that could no longer be tolerated and the next woman on the list was too ill to move into the apartment. Two persons' bad fortunes turned out to be our good fortune.

Driving home from work that night I contemplated telling Becky about her opportunity. Should I tell her right away? Should I wait until an opportune moment? Will she think I am rejecting her? What to do; what to do? I decided to just shout it out as soon as I walked in the door.

"Hey, Becky! Guess what? Manhattan has a room for you!"

"Oh, Goody!" she exclaimed and made a beeline for her bedroom.

Several minutes later the phone rang and it was Jim, a fellow I worked with at the hospital and who also coached our ladies' softball team. He had become one of Becky's buddies. I was surprised to hear his voice, because he had never called our home before. After our greeting one another, he said, "I didn't know you were moving to New York."

"Wherever did you get that idea?" I queried.

"Becky just called me and told me she's moving to Manhattan," he replied.

I assured him that Manhattan referred to the apartments for developmentally disabled adults on Manhattan Place in Boulder. No New York in our future. We both had a good chuckle.

The Phone

Becky learned to use the phone at age 20. That year the school presented a workshop on phone use and its importance. I had started working at the hospital in April 1981, and one day in the fall I was paged innumerable times. When I finally had time to answer the page, it was none other than my daughter Becky. She was so excited about reaching me and doing it all by herself. A person of my acquaintance happened to be in the hospital that day, and, upon encountering me asked me if I held a really important position on the staff. I informed her of my status and asked why she would think I held a position of importance.

"Well, I heard you paged so many times I thought you must be in a significant position," she answered. I assured her that I was a rookie recreation therapist in the rehab department and my position held no special status whatsoever. It was simply my daughter calling me and using her newfound skills.

When I got home that evening Pat Bach called me. Pat was the mother of Becky's best friend Donna. The conversation went as follows:

Pat: "Did Becky just learn to use the phone?"

Me: " Yes, she learned at school today."

Pat: " Well, don't you think *23* calls in one day is a bit much?"

Believe me I had a talk with Becky about the proper and polite use of the phone. We limited her to one call a day per household.

Within a few weeks Becky had several phone numbers memorized and made calls to each person daily when she got home from school. We had to make rules regarding the number of times one number could be called and the appropriate time to make those calls. Becky was an early riser and would call people at 5:00 a.m! It took only a couple of irate complaints before limits were set. It got to the point where we would warn people about giving their phone number to Becky. It became her social connection and still is to this day. She can remember a phenomenal list of phone numbers and calls them on a regular basis.

She would come home from work, fix a snack and then begin her phoning marathon every day. I don't know for sure how many people she'd call, but it had to be upwards of twenty. She calls me daily like clock-work and we discuss the weather, meals, people, work and I relate to her what we did that day. The conversation is pretty much verbatim from day to day. When I don't hear from her I worry that something is amiss.

Her ability to use the phone resulted in her 'mergency' call to neighbors when the basement flooded. It's a handy tool for her and, knowing that she can call and report an emergency gives me peace of mind that I would not otherwise have.

The Manhattan Apartments

Becky moved into the Manhattan Apartments in July 1985. Her counselor and case manager advised me to limit contact with her for the first two or three weeks. She needed time to adjust and they felt it would be better with minimal contact from me. Phone calls were encouraged, but not face-to-face visits.

After three weeks I called and asked if she'd like to go out to lunch and do some shopping.

"Hey, Yeah!" she responded with enthusiasm.

I picked her up and we headed for the mall. After picking up a few things that she wanted, we went to a restaurant called FOOD. She ordered a submarine sandwich and a diet Coke, her favorite beverage. While waiting for our meal to be prepared, I reminded Becky of a couple of things that had been cancelled due to the move.

"You need to get a haircut, and your counselor needs to re-schedule your dental appointment," I told her.

She looked at me, gave a big "TSKKK!" and said, "You're not my mother any more."

I burst out laughing. That was the last thing I expected to come out of her mouth. It was her way of telling me that I was no longer the boss. She was her own person and didn't need a mother to tell her what to do.

Peer pressure at Manhattan worked a minor miracle on Becky's habit of wetting the bed. Whether it was her chronic bladder infections as a

Becky all grown up

youngster or the brain damage, she had bed-wetting problems until she moved out our house.

I tried every means possible to change that behavior. 'Behavior Modification' was the buzzword used for bribery in those days. I started by offering her rewards if she could stay dry all night. It worked for a week. I then had to up the ante and offer more intriguing rewards. Each new upgrade was successful for about a week and then became old hat and routine.

Finally, I decided she should have to change her own sheets. We had a brief training session and she was on her own. The first day I came home from work she met me at the door and proudly announced, "Guess what, Mom? I changed my own sheets!" It was a source of self-esteem for her, and it didn't change the bed-wetting status.

The next step was to inform her that she would now have to launder her own bed linens. We put a piece of colored tape on the dial so she would know where to set it, did a brief training regarding water temperature and amounts of soap and other laundry additives, and she was off and running.

She met me at the door that next evening and announced with the same degree of pride, "Mom! I washed my own sheets!" She continued to have nocturnal accidents. What was a mother to do? I just accepted the fact that bed-wetting was part of who she was and I let go of my compulsion to solve this problem.

Within a month or two of living at the Manhattan Apartments she no longer wet the bed. Ahhhhh. Peer pressure. Sometimes it produces positive effects. It certainly did in our situation.

A Memorable Mother's Day

Within the year following Becky's move to Manhattan Place she called me. The phone rang and I answered with a cheerful 'Good Morning.'

"Hey, Mom! What're we doin' for Mother's Day this year?" she chirped with her usual enthusiasm for holidays.

I thought a minute and then said, "You know what, Becky? I'm the Mom. Why don't you plan something and let me know."

"Okay", she said. "I'll do that."

Mind you, Mother's Day had been celebrated every year at our house with my doing the cleaning, cooking, serving and cleaning up. It was not a chore, because it brought the family together which was always a joyful time. With all the kids out on their own, I decided in that quick minute that it was their turn to make the plans.

An hour later she called. "Guess what, Mom. We're going to Bananas on Mother's Day. 'Bout 12:00."

"Really?' I queried.

"Yah", she answered. "I called everybody and told them."

She called her sister, brother, grandmother and Mart, her grandma's husband. She did it all by herself.

As planned, we all met at Bananas, a local favorite restaurant in Boulder. Todd brought me a single rose. Cindy gave me a lovely card. Becky's card was the highlight of the afternoon, however. I opened it and smiled broadly and asked if she had chosen it herself. Of course, she had, *all* by herself.

The "Mother's Day" card

I handed it to her brother who couldn't control his laughter. You see, on the front of the card was a child's train loaded with presents and a cake and driven by an old-fashioned engineer. A squirrel is waving at the engineer, and colorful balloons are flying behind the train. It is fun and delightful, something that would catch her eye. The kicker was that the message said 'For a special Grandson. A maze for your birthday'.

The message inside, including a maze for me to attempt to traverse successfully, read,

'This birthday express is heading your way
with a big load of wishes for your happy day–
But just down the road it has to get by
an old broken-down bridge and a cliff–oh my!
But, Grandson, for sure it's going to get through
with a load full of wishes and love just for you.

HAPPY BIRTHDAY
HAVE FUN!

So obviously she can't read, but what fun that she can't. We all had a good laugh, and she didn't seem to be hurt by it. I still have the card after 28 years. It was a Mother's Day to remember.

Guardianship

Carmel House was a very successful living situation for about fifty developmentally disabled adults in Boulder County. It was an old fraternity house, had three floors and all the amenities a home should have. Ability levels and potential for independence divided the floors. The new residents moved in on the first floor and, as they improved and matured moved up a floor at a time. When they graduated from the third floor, they were ideally prepared for a more independent environment.

A gentleman named Jim was the director of Carmel House, and he was a very forward-thinking person. He believed with all his heart that his residents should have all the rights and privileges of any citizen and thus frowned upon the idea of guardianship. I listened and adhered to his message until the day he changed his mind.

Ideals and theories are fine on paper but sometimes don't work when put to practice in the real world. It seems a young stranger who was passionate about disabled people being their own persons came through Boulder on his way to a People First conference in Oregon. People First is a 'self-advocacy organization that was formed by, is run by, and exists for people with developmental disabilities...........' (www.missouripeoplefirst.org) He stopped by Carmel House and convinced the residents to take all their savings out of the bank and come with him to the conference.

Jim tried without success to discourage him from this action. He told the young man that the money was all they had and to deplete their savings accounts would not be beneficial for them. The young man insisted that they were their own persons and had their rights and no one could take them away. Empty their savings accounts they did, much to Jim's chagrin. At that point he let it be known that he thought guardianship under those circumstances was a good idea.

I thought about it for a while and decided I was going to become Becky's guardian in order to have control in three areas of her life; financial, medical and relationships, i.e. marriage. The financial is self-explanatory. Medically I wanted to be informed and consulted about any major medical issues that may arise. Regarding relationships, I wanted to be able to have a say in her marrying if that should ever be a probability. Thank goodness she is not the marrying kind. She loves men but is not a sexual being. She is more into being buddies than lovers.

The speech therapist at Ruth Wood School was also a lawyer. She studied law so she could be a legal advocate for the developmentally disabled students she taught. In fact, she was Becky's therapist for tongue thrusting, an abnormality that adversely affected her bite and thus her ability to eat. Mary Ann, the speech therapist/lawyer was more than willing to help me with guardianship of Becky.

We filled out all the forms and went before a judge who asked me a few pointed questions, apparently approved of my answers and granted me guardianship without any further discussion. Mary Ann would not take even a cent for her work for me. I will always be grateful for her expertise and willingness to help.

With each new counselor, new living situation, and new aspect of her life, I have to emphasize that she is her own spokesperson and decision maker when it comes to everyday issues. I don't need to be contacted about vacations or shopping or owning a cat. I reserve the right to have a say in only those three areas already mentioned. She truly is fiercely independent, and I have no desire to diminish that for any reason.

Manhattan Roommates

Becky's first roommate at Manhattan was a woman named Karen. Karen and I share the same birthday, though she is a year younger than I. She became Becky's best friend and still is today. She is on Becky's call list, and they talk daily.

Karen was the best roommate Becky had in all the years of sharing living space. Karen didn't try to boss Becky around, didn't steal from Becky, and was just a good friend.

Janice

When Karen moved out, Janice moved in. Janice had spent her entire life up to that point in the Grand Junction state institution. She had not been exposed to life on the outside and had some habits that were less than desirable. Janice had Down Syndrome, carrot-red hair, and was about five feet tall at the most. She was a voluptuous little lady.

She taught Becky how to shoplift. Now, I don't think they really knew that it was a crime; they just picked up things they liked and walked out of a store with them. They were apprehended at Safeway after a shoplifting spree and Becky was actually prohibited from entering the store for the next two years. I think that taught her a very difficult lesson.

One day when Becky was at work Janice went into her bedroom and took a paycheck from Hoshi Motors, Becky's place of employment. She was devious enough and clever enough to white out Becky's name and write her own in the 'pay to' field. Safeway, knowing Janice and trusting her at that time, cashed the check. I was incredulous. What business in its right mind would cash such an awkwardly assigned check? Janice was reprimanded by the staff and had to repay Becky every penny she took.

She may have been a kleptomaniac or she may have felt entitled to help herself to anything she saw that she liked. Maybe living in a state institution deprived her of the benefits of working and having spending money and thus she felt she deserved to have what others had. Who knows? At any rate, a lock was placed on Becky's bedroom door. What kind of living conditions requires one to carry a key to one's bedroom? Not the best situation, to say the least.

Janice was also a little sex kitten. She discovered that she could have any guy she wanted if she just provided him with sexual favors. She had more boyfriends than any girl I ever met. Of course, they were developmentally disabled like she was, but she had her pick of the crop.

One year Becky asked if she could have a sleepover at our house on New Year's Eve. She invited Janice, Lana and Donna. After dinner we retired to the family room to watch the New Year's festivities on TV. Around 10:00 Janice wandered down the hall to her assigned bedroom and came back wearing a low-cut lacy negligee, with more than a little cleavage showing. She knew how to attract attention.

Wally pushed himself out of the recliner, walked over to my chair and whispered in my ear, "I'm out of here. It's time for me to go to bed. I don't want her to get any ideas." And to bed he did go. He wasn't taking any chances on being falsely accused or presumed attracted to her.

All of this was way over Becky's head. She is probably what one might call asexual. She seems to have no inclination that way. She loves men,

l. to r. Lana, Janice, Becky, Donna

but as buddies and counselors, not as potential sexual partners. We did not invite Janice back to the house following that incident.

TERRY

Becky's next roommate was a young woman named Terry. She was non-verbal, overweight, unemployed, and had overlaying emotional problems. Her father began dating one of the young ladies in the apartment building and eventually married her. That might be an indication of the severity of Terry's dysfunction. Not only was Jessica, his wife, developmentally delayed, she was young enough to be his daughter. She carried a baby doll with her everywhere she went. It was a very strange coupling by all standards.

As an unemployed resident of the Manhattan Apartments, Terry was home all day. She, too, helped herself to Becky's money, belongings, toys and clothing. Again, Becky had to lock her bedroom door. Because of Terry's inability to speak and relate to others, there was no possibility of developing a relationship with her. Becky isolated herself in her bedroom and only came out at mealtime.

Regardless of these less-than-acceptable roommates, Becky thrived at Manhattan and loved her independence. She was a favorite of the counselors and they would include her in their own activities.

One counselor named Julie liked and trusted Becky so much that she would take Becky with her on her errand runs and leave her in the car to watch her infant. Becky and Julie and Hailey are friends to this day.

LISA

The straw that broke the camel's back was a young woman with Down Syndrome who was quite verbal and equally precocious. In her defense, her parents might as well have abandoned her at birth. She was a source of embarrassment for them. Her father was a successful lawyer and her mother a thriving real estate agent. They plied her with all her material needs and wishes but ignored her emotional needs.

When she was in school and Special Olympics, she drove her teachers and coaches crazy with her manipulative demands for attention. Her banter was constant and never-ending. She grew into a young woman and along the route to adulthood she, like Janice, discovered that she could gain the attention she craved by providing sexual favors for young men in the developmentally disabled population.

When she moved into the Manhattan Apartments a young man named Ed was residing in one of the ground level units. He was well known for his sexual adventures, all legal, consensual and above board, as far as I know. The young women he courted for sexual activities were more than eager to satisfy his needs. Lisa became one of his consorts.

He had a fetish for 'boobs.' Becky, in spite of her size and tomboyish ways, had huge breasts. She always wore t-shirts and sweatshirts in a large size, not specifically to camouflage her body, but because they were comfortable. Oftentimes she was mistaken for being a male. She is six feet tall, large boned, has broad shoulders, which taper down to a small butt and long skinny legs. She wears her hair very short and certainly appears more boyish than feminine.

Living in the same building it didn't take Ed long to discover Becky was very buxom. Within a few weeks he and Lisa began harassing Becky about posing topless for Ed's camera. Thank goodness she knew enough to say no. That didn't discourage him, though, and one day her counselor called to fill me in on the situation. I begged her to keep a close eye on them and to monitor any activity that might include the whole house.

A few weeks later she called with 'good news' and 'bad news.' It seems Lisa managed to manipulate or threaten the residents, one at a time, into buying her lunch or other items. When it became Becky's 'turn' to take Lisa out they found themselves at Ed's new apartment. He had been able to move into an unsupervised apartment facility closer to town.

They entered the apartment and Ed immediately began pressing Becky to take off her shirt so he could photograph her breasts. She said 'No way!" Then he and Lisa proceeded to strip down and engage in sexual intercourse right there in front of Becky and the world.

Becky stormed out of the door saying in a loud voice, "I'm outta here!" She walked the brief mile back to her apartment and told her counselor what had happened. The good news was that Becky had the presence of mind to walk away.

At that point I gave the counselor an ultimatum. Find another place for Lisa to live or move Becky to another facility. My feeling was that she had maintained her innocence up to this point and did not need to be put in those inappropriate situations. The counselor agreed and put the wheels into motion to make it happen.

The last I heard about Lisa she was living in a host home and needed constant supervision. It seems a few years later she had molested a child and was put under lock and key to prevent any future such occurrences, and she is listed as a sexual predator. I guess I need to thank my lucky stars that we found out about her when we did.

A Case of Mistaken Identity

When Becky was in her early 30's we took her to a basketball game at the University of Colorado. We found our seats and Wally wanted to get a beer. Becky informed us she needed to go to the bathroom. While Wally was in line for beer, Becky went to the ladies' room. I was waiting in the middle of the passage way for both when I noticed a policeman outside the women's bathroom. He looked hesitant to go in, and knowing in my heart what he was doing there, I sauntered up to him and asked, "What's going on?"

"Oh, apparently there's some guy in the ladies' room."

"I can assure you that it is my daughter. She is very boyish and often taken for a guy. She is definitely a female. I would be willing to bet you $100 that's what's going on."

Sure enough, Becky walked out and I introduced her to the policeman. He smiled and continued on his beat.

Cottonwood Apartments

Imagine, the new name for the Boulder County Board for Disabilities, had contracted with an apartment complex north of Boulder to rent six or seven units for their special clients. It was felt that the easiest way to separate Becky and Lisa was to move Becky. She had not had a successful living situation at the Manhattan Apartments, at least regarding acceptable roommates. It was time for a new environment.

She was to room with an older woman named Elaine. Elaine seemed quiet and capable and compatible. They worked well together. Each had her own bedroom and they shared a bathroom, kitchen and living room. Unlike the routine at the Manhattan Apartments where they took turns cooking dinner, these ladies did their own individual shopping and food preparation. It required cooperation for them to share the kitchen facilities and they seemed to be able to work that out amicably.

It worked well until family members decided that Becky should have a cat. A grand niece of my stepfather had baby kittens and was looking for homes for them. Becky's sister and my mother went through all the proper channels to get permission for Becky to have a cat. Becky named the cat Rocky. He was an adorable black kitten with a white spot on his chest.

The only channel they didn't go through was to check with Elaine to see how she felt about cats. She hated them. Because it was her apartment first, she had the final say, and Rocky was relegated to live his life in Becky's bedroom. He, his food, his litter box, his bed and toys were confined to a ten-foot by ten-foot space. He existed that way four years until Becky moved to the Timberridge apartments.

By an uncanny coincidence, Elaine's 'boyfriend' was none other than the infamous, promiscuous sex idol Ed. We had moved Becky to the Cottonwood Apartments to get away from him. I called Imagine and insisted that he not be allowed in the apartment with Becky. If Elaine wanted to see him outside of the apartment that was not my business, but I felt that he should be forbidden to be anywhere near Becky. They agreed to oversee that situation.

Within a year of Becky's moving in with Elaine, Elaine became quite ill. After several doctors' appointments and hospitalizations, no diagnosis was determined. Eventually she moved to Oklahoma to live with her sister. We never officially found out what the cause of her illness was. My take on it is that it probably was AIDS. If she was sexually active with Ed, as I'm sure she must have been, aids could have been a distinct possibility. I would bet money that young man never felt the need to use protection.

BILL

Becky was not ready to live by herself yet, so the powers that be decided that she and Bill would be a good match. Bill was a young man who had gone to school with Becky. He graduated maybe two years before she did. When his family still lived in Boulder they lived down the street from us. He was another whose family just sustained him financially and physically but spent no quality time with him.

When he discovered we lived in his neighborhood, he would often stroll by our house in hopes of finding someone outside. Invariably we would invite him in for milk and cookies or a snack of some kind. One Easter we were preparing to dye eggs and invited him in to help. He was elated.

I had an Easter egg hunt for Becky until she was in her late thirties. It was really more fun for me than it was for her. Anyway, we loved Bill. He was a big lovable teddy bear type.

Now this many years later he was to be Becky's roommate at the Cottonwood Apartments. My mother came unglued when she found out Becky was to have a male roommate. I assured my mother they were both asexual and that the living situation would be completely platonic. She finally settled down and accepted the notion after she met Bill and watched their interactions.

Bill had a cell phone. He could use it like any young person can. He was very adept at mechanical things and soon became very bossy with Becky. Now, bossy people are Becky's pet peeve. There are ways to convince her to do things, but certainly not by demanding or seeming superior and bossy. Their roommate situation began deteriorating and after a couple of years they were moved to different living situations. She had lived at Cottonwood for four years.

Bill was grossly overweight, and the staff decided he needed more dietary supervision. He was moved to a host home. Becky, on the other hand, was allowed to have her very own apartment at the new Timberridge facility. The staff decided she had made sufficient progress in independent living and deserved to try living on her own. The apartments were close to the University of Colorado, and many CU students resided in the complex. The bus line ran right by her apartment, so getting to work would be a piece of cake.

From the rumors we heard, Bill lost nearly 100 pounds at the host home. I'm sure I'd not recognize him if I passed him on the street.

A Self-serving Counselor

One of Becky's counselors at Cottonwood was an older woman named Jan. She really enmeshed herself in Becky's life. At first I thought it was great that she cared so much for Becky and her welfare. It turns out she was an opportunist.

Becky had nice bedroom furniture when she moved into the Cottonwood apartment. It never entered my mind that she might need new furnishings. Jan wrote me a note telling me that they had purchased a new bed and dresser for her. Her old bed had drawers underneath which took care of storage for a lot of her 'collectibles.' The old bed was a double bed, which suited her size. I didn't question the motives; I just figured Jan knew what was best.

Becky found herself with a large check due to underpayment from Social Security. Jan called and asked if she could take Becky to Disneyland with the money.

"Of course," I said. " Becky would love that."

Plans were made. Vacations were requested from her boss. Travel and hotel reservations were made and the two of them were off to California. Becky had a marvelous time. Pictures of her with all the Disney characters, swimming in the pool with her favorite doll, attending shows and special programs fill an album. I was so happy that she was able to do that.

Becky and Minnie Mouse at Disneyland

Then I found out that she paid Jan's way. I was furious; not so much that she had paid for Jan's expenses, but that Jan did not tell me that up front. Something so simple and required by Imagine would have made all the difference in my attitude. To add to my frustration with this woman, I found out that she took the furniture that had been replaced for her own personal use. It turns out the furniture she bought was not nearly as good quality as the furniture it replaced.

I, who seldom find reason to complain about anything regarding Becky's care and treatment, raised a stink about this woman and her sneaky ways. Soon after that she was fired. I guess people like that are always looking for someone or something they can use for their own advantage.

I am happy to say that was the first and last time a counselor has done anything like that while assigned to Becky's care. I must learn to not be so trusting in the future.

Diabetes

In the mid-nineties Becky was diagnosed with Type II diabetes. She already was taking meds for high cholesterol and high blood pressure, so diabetes prescriptions were added to her regimen. She had 'finger-sticks' twice a week and had to watch her diet. Lucky for her, it was a mild case and didn't require insulin shots. It took a while for her to understand that her sugar and carbohydrate intake had to be limited; not just a little, but a lot.

Remarkably, she cut back on her sweets and within a year or so the finger-sticks were discontinued. She was required, however, to continue taking oral insulin and having regular check-ups.

After moving into the host homes, she has lost a lot of weight and the doctors have discontinued most of her medications. She is healthier than she's been in a long while.

Timberridge

Becky moved into Timberridge in 2006, an apartment complex very close to the University of Colorado. Imagine had contracted for about thirteen units and the rest were occupied by CU students. They were located on the bus route she used to get to work. Her placement there seemed to be appropriate for her needs and her level of independence.

Her case manager decided, without any consultation with anyone, to put Becky in an upstairs apartment. Probably fifteen steps up a very narrow stairway led to Becky's residence. She had to ascend and descend those steps with her backpack at least twice a day. She had to carry her trash receptacle down those stairs once a week, not to mention laundry and groceries and whatever else she might need.

When I realized this I became very concerned and called Imagine to ask whose idea it was to place her on the second level. It turns out her case manager, a young, idealistic woman named Katy, thought it would be good exercise for her to walk up and down the stairs several times a day.

I insisted, I mean really insisted, that they get her on the ground floor. Her balance had been a minor problem all her life, but after she turned forty it just seemed to gradually get worse. They held me in high enough esteem to listen to my request and within a week she was re-situated on the first level.

I love Imagine's programs, and I trust them implicitly to do what is best for their clients. However, I have had my issues now and then. In general, I am not a complainer. I pick and choose my battles.

It was reported to me in the spring that a young man had stopped by Becky's apartment to take her to a class on social behavior and etiquette. As Becky came out the front door of her apartment he noticed a distinct odor of gas. He hurried her out of the apartment and called the manager. The Timberridge apartments had gas stoves!! Imagine that? Putting developmentally disabled adults in apartments with gas stoves. Whose hare-brained idea was that? They use microwaves for cooking.

I was assured that the stove had been disconnected and the gas shut off to her apartment. Trusting that Imagine had indeed taken the necessary measures to make Becky's environment safer, I didn't give it another thought. That is until July of that year. Wally and I had gone to the Front Range to celebrate my mother's birthday and were picking Becky up for church on a Sunday morning. She opened the door a crack to see who was there, and the smell of gas hit me like a brick. I pulled her out and pushed the door open as wide as possible. By some stroke of good fortune she had her window open for ventilation or we might have found her unconscious or even dead.

I marched to the counselors' office and, short of screaming, let them know in a few choice words that I expected something to be done and done immediately. When we returned I asked to see the gas hookup to make sure this time it had been disconnected. It had been. Upon returning home I wrote a scathing letter to the supervisor of residential services. I hope my ranting maybe saved others from the effects of careless oversight.

Independent Living

Becky thrived living on her own at Timberridge. The apartment was a one bedroom with a bathroom, living room, and efficiency kitchen. Rocky settled right in and made himself at home. He remained an indoor cat while Becky lived there, getting out once in a while on a leash with Becky in tow.

She did her own meal preparation, packing her lunch for work every night before going to sleep. Her breakfasts consisted of yogurt and cereal; lunch was a peanut butter and jelly sandwich and fruit, and dinner was a Healthy Choice TV dinner. She was so happy and content having her own space and truly being her own boss. Her favorite thing about living there was being in charge of herself. No one to boss her around.

She took the city bus to and from her job at Hoshi Motors. She did her own laundry and grocery shopping. She was reliable when it came to taking her 'pills.' She had to take medication for diabetes, cholesterol and high blood pressure. Her apartment looked like a bomb had landed there. She was never much of a neat freak.

The most important thing was that it was her space and her responsibility, and she could do whatever she wanted with no one to tell her otherwise. She loved it. The staff loved her because she was intensely independent and usually easy-going. She was a prime example of what independent living could be for her population.

I can't count the times I've said, "Had anyone told me when she was little the day would come when she would be living alone, taking care of herself and a cat independently, I would have told them they were crazy."

I felt that she could live successfully with a roommate whose strengths complemented hers. They could help each other out and work cooperatively to make independent living a combined effort. Here she was at age 46 living in her very own apartment.

Her life blossomed at Timberridge. She agreed to a second job with Labor Source, the vocational department at Imagine. For years they had been trying to convince her to take on a second job to supplement her income. She worked only two days a week at Hoshi Motors and had a lot of spare time for watching TV. The staff wanted her to occupy her time with more worthwhile activities.

New counselors finally developed a weekend activity program involving outings in the community. Becky never missed an opportunity to participate. They loved her for her enthusiasm and willingness to get involved in whatever the activity might be.

Employment

Becky's first real job with pay was at the Boulder County Humane Society. She loves animals and was so excited about working in a place where there were so many dogs and cats. In our finite minds we pictured her feeding the animals, brushing their coats, and walking the dogs or playing 'fetch'. In reality the job consisted of Becky's cleaning cages. Not a fun job! Not fun at all.

My memory of why the job terminated after a few months is vague, but it did. From that job she moved on to Boulder Manor Health Care facility. It, too, sounded like a great job for someone with Becky's limited abilities. She was to fill water pitchers, help change bed linens, and take needed supplies to patients' rooms. She started the job with that job description, and it worked well for her until the day they needed help in the dining room.

They were not aware that Becky was unable to read. As mentioned earlier, she can read 'Men' and 'Women,' bus numbers, familiar names, but basically cannot read. There is a major disconnect in her brain that interferes with learning reading and math, writing and spelling. No amount of money or education will ever change that fact. Somewhere in her records it must state, "Becky cannot read."

Nursing home residents have different dietary restrictions depending on their health and their weight. No one explained to Becky that she needed to give the correct tray to the correct resident. She just delivered them willy-nilly to one patient after another. Diabetics got dessert; sodium-restricted residents got salt and other sodium-laden foods; vegetarians got meat. She was fired on the spot.

The vocational counselors placed her at the new Boulder Salad Company restaurant on opening day. She was to be a dishwasher. Simple enough, don't you think? Stand in one place and load the dishwasher. Sounded like a job she could handle. She might have gotten bored to death with it in time but was never given the opportunity to find out. She lasted one day.

Customers came in droves and additional help was required to keep things moving smoothly. They sent Becky into the fray to buss tables. I have mentioned more than once that balance was one of Becky's biggest problems. So, put her in a crowded room with tables and chairs situated close together, give her a tub for *glassware* and expect her to do the job without fail. I don't know how many tubs she may have carried to the back successfully, but one was all it took for her to drop after stumbling in the bustling dining area. The glassware shattered and twenty stitches later Becky was fired.

She tried her hand at Wendy's, a job that didn't last too long. That Wendy's was closed soon after she started. She did a stint at the University of Colorado Memorial Center where she and a crew of workers wrapped silverware and replenished the utensils on the salad bar. One day it was noticed that Becky picked her nose and failed to wash her hands. That was contrary to the Health Department's regs, so she was fired.

McDonalds was added to Becky's resume. Her duties were emptying the trash, putting in new trash bags, picking up trays, wiping tables, pushing in chairs. It was mostly janitorial duty, and she was very capable of doing a good job without the restrictions of illiteracy and hand washing.

The owner of McDonalds was a family friend. That did not play into Becky's getting the job. It did, however, play into her keeping it as long as she did. She had a young supervisor, a blond woman named Sandy who didn't seem much brighter than Becky, if I can be so bold as to judge. My sense was that Becky was a source of frustration for her. There weren't any obvious problems, though, until Sandy changed shifts and Becky was left unsupervised. The owner called me one day and said, "We're a little concerned about Becky's job performance. She just isn't doing the job the way we'd like her to."

I asked if anything had changed since she started. He told me her supervisor had a different schedule and couldn't oversee Becky's duties personally. I asked how Becky was expected to know what her duties were without someone there to direct her. He replied, "Oh, Sandy leaves her notes."

"Well, Bob," I remarked. "Becky can't read."

He had no idea she was unable to read. Who was in charge of her placement anyway? Didn't they have her records and didn't they give them to her employer so that the employer would know her abilities and limitations?

Accepting that information he decided to keep her on the job. He eventually turned the store over to his son to manage. The son had no patience for Becky, and again I got a call from the owner. His concern was that she was shirking her duties and avoiding work of any kind. I asked him if he reprimanded her as he did his other employees who failed to complete their assignments.

"Oh, I couldn't do that," he stated.

"And why not?" I asked.

"Well, you know, because she has problems, and I just wouldn't feel right about it."

"How else is she going to learn to get along in this world if she is not treated the same way you would treat any employee. She has to learn to live by the same rules. It is not fair to her to let her get away with disobedience."

"I never thought of that," He said.

She lasted another six months and was let go. Unemployed again, but not for long.

Toby

Through a special grant Becky was hired to be a teacher's aide for a young disabled boy named Toby. Toby had cerebral palsy and was confined to a wheelchair. He was non-verbal and wore diapers. He needed help with meals and diaper changing. After Senate bill 94-142 passed in Congress, most special education students were mainstreamed into the regular schools, so Toby was a student at Fairview High School in Boulder, Colorado. Burke School was to be no more. No more segregation of special needs students.

Becky became his fulltime companion while he was at school. She pushed his wheelchair from class to class, fed him at lunchtime, and changed his diapers when necessary. Of course, all this was done with close supervision.

The following is a letter I received from the teacher who was Becky's supervisor on this job:

"Dear Holly,

This is an official' notice that Becky did a <u>FANTASTIC</u> job today! She was quick to listen and perform a job and did a fine job on everything. She's learning *a lot already – helping do the laundry – in the bathroom, and assisting children in tasks.*

On Tuesday's Becky can meet us at the pool if that's easier for you. I sent her on a #3 bus and she sounded confident that she could make it home O.K.

So, we'll see you both tomorrow. Have a nice evening.

Carol"

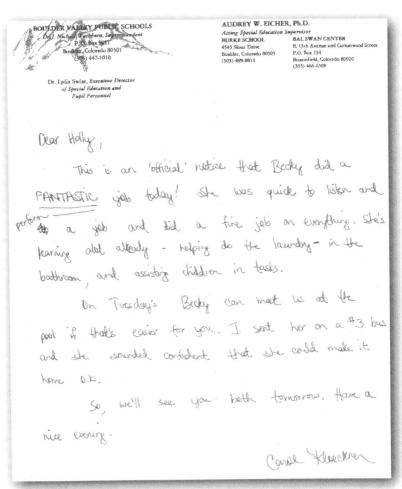

Letter of commendation from Becky's supervisor

She and Toby became fast friends. His face would light up whenever he saw her. The grant ran out at the end of the school year. Becky actually made a decent salary on that job. It was another step toward maturity and independence, a level I never thought possible when she was a youngster. What do mothers know, anyway?

Hoshi Motors

In the fall of 1981 I was driving a small, white Honda Civic. We had acquired it by trading our Cadillac Seville to my folks for the Honda and a cash payment. It was not in the best condition, but it would do to get me to work everyday. Don was working in Colorado Springs at the time, so it was my car.

One particularly cold October day it had difficulty starting. I decided it needed to be worked on and looked for a Honda repair shop near the hospital where I worked. There was one on 8th Street about ten blocks from Memorial Hospital. I parked in front of the garage, filled out the necessary paper work, and they assured me that it would be ready at the end of the workday. When I picked it up the mechanic came to speak to me about it. The mechanic was a woman!! A woman named Laurie who, as it turned out, *loved* working on cars. She told me nothing made her happier than to take an old run down Honda and make it purr. She also told me what a disappointment she was to her father. He wanted her to go to college and become some kind of professional.

She had my business! I took that little Honda to her until it had to be sold. In the meantime, I had raved about her to my folks, who owned two Hondas. They lived in Southeast Denver and drove fifty miles to bring their Hondas to Laurie, who now was the proud owner of Hoshi Motors.

Hoshi became the most popular Honda repair shop in Boulder. What a treat to find a shop where the mechanics loved what they did and could not do less than an excellent job. Laurie had very high standards and thousands of repeat customers, including my mother and stepfather.

My mother had retired after working for the Colorado State Employment Service for thirty-seven years. She knew about creating jobs and finding work for people. They always picked Becky up and took her to lunch when they were in Boulder for work on their cars. Oftentimes they took Becky into Hoshi with them to pay the bill, so Becky was no stranger to Laurie.

One day in 1991 Laurie happened to mention to Mother that she was thinking of hiring someone to do simple janitorial tasks around the shop a couple of days a week. The light bulb in Mother's head flashed on and she suggested that Laurie might want Becky to come work for her. The wheels were set in motion and within a few weeks Becky was a full-fledged employee of Hoshi Motors, complete with a Hoshi mechanics uniform that had the logo on the shirt pocket. She started on August 20, 1991.

She worked Tuesday and Thursday from 9:30 to 12:30 every week and loved it. Not only was the job one that Becky could handle, the entire staff loved her and she loved Laurie's dogs that spent the day in the shop sleeping in the sun. She was in her element.

Laurie paid Becky minimum wage beginning at $5.25 an hour and gave her raises over the years. When she left Hoshi's she was making $7.25 an hour, the going minimum wage at that time. Becky's responsibilities included taking out the oil and the trash, sweeping the garage, washing windows, wiping down the counters, cleaning the bathroom, and keeping the stairway clear of clutter.

Laurie is a special employer. Most of the mechanics who started with her back in the 80's are still at Hoshi today. Brandon, who started working there the same time Becky did, was Becky's favorite. They just hit it off. They loved to tease each other and play practical jokes and when Becky landed in the hospital he came to see her. She walked in the Bolder Boulder for eight years in a row and Brandon was always on the sidelines cheering her on.

Becky never tired of her job at Hoshi. She worked there for 22 years. They celebrated her birthday every year and made her feel like she was truly part of the staff, which she was. She no longer works there due to an accident that does not allow her to work or walk without a walker, and a walker isn't conducive to performing the job required.

Laurie has since retired and *gave* the business to Brandon. She still works there part time, but he owns and runs the business. No one does that these days. She is truly a unique woman.

Wrapping Silverware

In 2005 Becky's Labor Source counselor convinced Becky to take a second job. Who knows what devices Marsha used to sign Becky up for two more workdays? I thought it would never happen. Labor Source had tried for years to put Becky in an additional worksite, all to no avail. Her perpetual response was, "I like my life the way it is!"

Now, out of the clear blue sky she decides she wants a second job. She was assigned a job wrapping silverware for Johnny Carino's, an Italian restaurant in Longmont, Colorado, a twenty-mile bus ride from her apartment. Labor Source rode the bus with her until they felt she was comfortable doing it independently. Labor Source is an independent vocational/rehabilitation entity that works with Imagine in job placement and job supervision. Within a few days Becky was riding the bus by herself.

She started rolling silverware for Carino's at $2.84 and hour and within three months her salary was raised to $3.12. After six months and receiving the title of 'champion silverware roller,' she was given a $.34 raise. The job at Carino's ended in March 2007 when the job site was terminated.

She had expressed an interest in working at another restaurant and the search was started. In the meantime she worked for G & S recycling dismantling electronics for re-distribution; the Flower Bin nursery in Longmont in a seasonal position, and In-Clover dog food company packaging organic dog biscuits.

Labor Source managed to get a contract for rolling silverware with the Rock Bottom Restaurant and the Chop House in Boulder. Because

Becky had moved to her own apartment in the interim, Labor Source had to provide transportation. So on Wednesdays and Fridays she was picked up and taken to work with the 'crew,' her term for her fellow workers. She loved the job and especially loved having lunch with all her buddies on the 'crew'. She maintained the title of 'champion silverware roller' though the job also included cleaning her work area, polishing knives, and taking the finished silverware to the shelves. She was required to leave her work area ready for the next day's workers.

Rock Bottom eventually terminated the contract and Becky found work at The Outback Restaurant, which became her favorite place to work. She continued as a 'silverware roller' until November 2013, when her living situation disallowed transportation to the job.

Becky's resume would be lengthy. She has had a variety of experiences, and there will be more to come. Labor Source does an amazing job finding work for disabled folks in Boulder County, and Becky has been the recipient of their hard work and dedication. As I re-read her employment experiences I am amazed at what she has accomplished as a developmentally disabled adult who cannot read or write but who functions with success and grace in these trying times.

Birthdays

Birthdays were always a big deal when I was growing up. My Mother was a single mom, or might as well have been, until I was ten. My father went overseas when I was four, returned when I was six, and they divorced when I was seven. She didn't remarry until I was ten. She often worked more than one job to make ends meet, and my Grandmother, with whom we lived, was our caretaker. I didn't know until I was in my sixties that my mother had paid her to watch over us.

My mother always made sure that our birthdays were celebrated with a party and presents and friends. She would bake her famous high altitude chocolate cake, serve it with ice cream and candles, and invite all our little friends over to help us celebrate. Each party was complete with a birthday spanking; a custom I don't think is done anymore. It certainly wasn't painful and always fun while everyone counted out the years.

When I had children I carried out the custom I had grown up with. Every year each of my children celebrated a birthday with a party. I loved having all their friends at the house, singing happy birthday, blowing out the candles after making a wish, and opening the presents, which was the best part. When Becky's brother and sister reached their teenage years, they no longer wanted the usual birthday party. They celebrated with friends in their own way. We had a birthday cake and ice cream for dessert after a special dinner of their choosing. Except for Becky.

To this day we celebrate her birthday with friends and cake and presents. She calls me about mid-July and asks, "Hey, Mom. What're we doin' for my birthday? I can't b'lieve I'm gonna be 54. How old are you?" "76" I tell her. Her response? "Oh, my God!"

I remind her that it's a little early to be planning; her birthday is September 5th, and then I ask her what she wants to do. She will blurt out the name of a restaurant and then we make the guest list. It changes a little bit each year, but is basically the same: her Dad and his girlfriend, her brother and family, her sister and kids, Grandma and Mart when they were still living, Marsha, her Labor Source counselor, and friend Karen, her first roommate and still best friend and Karen's caregiver, her Uncle Keith and Pati, my friend, Holly. Now we will add her caregivers and kids in her host home.

I write an invitation, usually in poetic form, and mail it out about a month in advance. I wait patiently for the replies and then call the restaurant with a number. It is usually between 15 and 20. They graciously tell me they will be ready for us when we arrive. We take up the better part of a room with all the bodies and gifts that arrive. It is great fun, and the restaurant is most willing to light the candles and help us sing 'Happy Birthday.' Every year Becky gets so excited when that happens, almost like it's the first time.

In the early days when she lived at the Manhattan apartments and we still lived in Boulder, we had the gathering in the backyard. We grilled hamburgers and hot dogs and had potato salad and beans and all the trimmings. The birthday cake was always homemade and never a crumb was left after serving all the guests.

The most memorable year was the year we had a piñata. Her counselors bought it and hung it from a pole. It was a most lifelike black spider monkey, typically made of papier-mâché and full of candy and treats. Each of Becky's friends took a turn, put on the blindfold and the broom handle was placed in their hands. They swung at the piñata wildly while the rest of us made sure no one got hurt. It was futile. No one came near breaking it open. Finally we decided to let them try without blindfolds. It was a tough little bugger; not about to break easily.

Becky and the pinata

When it was Becky's turn she took the broom handle and went after that piñata with a vengeance. She knocked it down and it still didn't break open. Then she began beating it mercilessly. It was really hard to watch, even though we were all laughing so hard we were crying. It was hard to watch because it looked so realistic. Finally it cracked and all the entrails were available for the taking. A mad scramble ensued, and it didn't take long at all for the guests to fill their bags with the goodies. Sidling up to her counselor, I quietly suggested that next time they get a piñata that was not so lifelike. To this day I wish we had recorded the whole episode.

Becky still surprises me with her ability to problem-solve. Her friend Karen had moved since the prior year, and I had no idea how to get her new address. Becky also wanted an invitation sent to Karen's caregiver. Again, I had no address. I made numerous phone calls with no success. Becky, who calls me daily just to chat, called and said, "Hey, Mom. I know what we can do. You send the invitations to me and I'll give them to Karen. How about that?"

"Whoa! Becky," I replied. "What a great idea!"

And it was; and she thought of it all by herself. She would still meet Karen at the bus depot in the mornings before they went to their respective jobs. Good thinking, don't you agree?

She now lives with a host family, and we will still have a big birthday party with even more people next year. I have as much fun as she does. In so many ways it is a joy to have a child whose innocent sense of fun is intact after all these years. She would still believe in Santa if we would let her.

Individualized Planning Meetings

IEP or IP meetings have been part of Becky's life since she went to North Broadway School in 1971. By law the school was required to have an IEP or Individual Education Plan formulated every year Becky was in school.

It was a time to look at achievement and set new goals for the coming year.

Once Becky was under the auspices of Imagine, formerly the Boulder County Board for Developmental Disabilities (BCBDD), the onus fell on them to develop an annual IP or Individualized Plan for her. It became a really significant event in her life. She always hoped it would be 'good'. Again it was formulated to set goals for her in several categories, residential, health, safety, vocational, social. The discussion centered on how well she had done the prior year and the setting of new goals for the coming year.

The largest conference room was reserved for Becky's IP. She held the record for having the most attendees. Besides her counselor, case manager, vocational counselor, nurse and residential supervisor, there were her mother, stepfather, father and his girlfriend, brother Todd and wife Sarah. I was told at one point that there were clients who had no one come for the IP. Becky is lucky to have such an involved and caring family. The conference itself would last about an hour with lots of discussion and input from all parties. Finally, we would all sign off and then go out to lunch afterwards. It was always a major event in Becky's life.

Living five hours away, I promised I would be there for her IP's as long as I could drive safely and was healthy and strong enough to do so. Now, due to circumstances beyond anyone's control, Becky's IP's are held in late December, a time I choose not to drive over the mountain passes. I am now included via a conference call, which works well for me, and Becky seems to accept the reality of the situation. She still had most of the entourage there, with her host family more than filling in for my absence.

SSI

When Becky was 19 years old I was reminded that she was eligible for SSI, Supplemental Security Income, a form of social security for disabled persons. My lack of knowledge assumed that she would not be eligible for it until she moved out of the home. In spite of that, I decided to fill out the paperwork so it would be ready and available for the day that her eligibility was valid.

I painstakingly filled it out and sent it in to the Social Security Administration (SSA). Lo and behold, within six months she received a check for nearly $6,000. I was blown away. I deposited it in a bank account and then began making phone calls. There was no way I was going to start spending it before I knew it was truly there for her to spend. It seems there was a category called 'living in the home of another' which applied to Becky, since she was 19 years old, and it went into effect when one turned 18. The check was so big because it was made retroactive to her 18th birthday. The money was legally hers and could be used for her living expenses.

SSI checks began coming in monthly. Yearly they would send what seemed like reams of paperwork for me to fill out. They had something to do with Becky's continuing eligibility. One of the financial sections asked the amount of Becky's fair share of the household expenses, i.e. utilities, telephone, mortgage, etc. I sort of pulled a number out of the air that seemed fair to me. Before long we started getting notices that Becky was being overpaid and would we please refund 'X' amount to the SSA.

Refund I did and the notices kept coming. I became paranoid about spending any of her money because I didn't know when the next notice of overpayment might come and how much it might be.

Finally, I decided that I was doing something incorrectly. I called Social Security to make an appointment with a counselor. The cute little receptionist offered to answer my questions. I told her in no uncertain terms did I want to hear from her. I wanted to sit down across the table from someone who was in the know, look him or her in the eyes and have them tell me specifically how to figure out Becky's fair share. She meekly made an appointment for me and probably hoped against hope that she wouldn't be on duty when this irate, unreasonable woman came into the office.

I sat across the table from a very nice lady who calmly and with quiet assurance told me that Becky's fair share was a percentage of the actual amount spent on the household. In other words I should take all the expenses, divide them by the number of persons living in the house, and the result would be her fair share. How simple can that be? Now, I ask, why in the world isn't that written somewhere in the instructions for filling out all that paperwork?

Once I used that 'formula' for determining Becky's fair share, guess what? She had been <u>underpaid</u> for months, so we had another large check to deal with soon after that information was relayed.

Over the years Becky has received a number of large checks for being underpaid for a period of time. I used to get the paperwork from the SSA showing how her payments were determined. At one point I looked at them closely, being one of those people who often file things without reading them. I assume that they are correct and look no further. Well, this time I glanced at her income and couldn't believe my eyes. They had her monthly income at $795. Where in the world did that figure come from?

She worked six hours a week at Hoshi motors for $7.25 an hour. She worked 12 hours a week at the restaurants for $3.46 an hour. You do the math. At most her monthly salary would have been somewhere in the vicinity of $340 a month. I called the person in charge of monitoring income and SSI at Imagine to inquire about the whys and wherefores of her monthly income, was assured that she would look into it and told that, since I was not Becky's payee, I should not be getting that information from SSA, and thus no longer do. I have asked that they keep me informed if something is that far off the charts. I assume they will.

One year Becky received a check for underpayment for about seven years. The check was for more than $11,000. And, thanks to government regs, it had to be spent within six months. Folks on SSI cannot have more than $2,000 in savings, so they have to spend money whether they need anything or not. Becky has had a new TV every other year for the last eight years or so. Nothing wrong with the old ones, we just had to spend the money on something to keep her savings at the $2,000 limit.

We took the $11,000 check and went to a very expensive furniture store in Longmont, Colorado and bought whatever Becky wanted without looking at the price tags. I've never been in that situation before. I've always been one to compare, or wait for a sale or get it second hand. This was a new experience for me, and I must say I enjoyed it thoroughly. We bought her a new sofa, end table, kitchen chairs and a beautiful bedroom set. They were expensive, but when subtracted from the total amount we had to spend, there was still $6,000 in the kitty.

I pondered the situation for a brief minute or two and then asked Becky if she would like to take a vacation and include her brother and Sarah and their kids. "Hey, Yeah!!" She said without hesitation.

"Where do you want to go?"

"**BRANSON Missouri!**" She shouted.

So Branson it was. We invited Todd and Sarah and Carlin and Wiley, rented a van and headed out the next March. Branson or Bust! Todd and Sarah were delighted to be part of the entourage.

Branson

I knew very little about Branson, Missouri. The trip there was without incident and two days after leaving Boulder we arrived in the showplace of the 'Show Me' state. What a fun place to go!

There was anything and everything to do. We should have planned to stay two weeks instead of five days. We rented a condo near a lake and had about a 20-minute drive to the fun stuff. Shows galore, restaurants and more: putt-putt golf, sailing, boating, hiking, games, shopping, festivals, museums all there for the seeing and playing.

Unfortunately, Carlin was only 20 months old and not feeling well. It sort of interfered with Sarah's ability and willingness to have a good time. Any mother would have felt the same. We did see a Beatles show the first night there. It was amazing how much the performers not only looked like the original Beatles, they sounded like them to a tee. As the show progressed the audience got more and more into the atmosphere of the era, and by the end of the show we were all dancing in the aisles. Becky was right in the middle of it all boogying with the best of them.

We ate at terrific restaurants. One night we were sitting in a booth waiting to order and Todd looked at me and asked, "Mom, Can I have a steak?'

"You can have anything on the menu you want!" I answered.

Again, I've never been in that position. It was a fun feeling. I felt like lady got rocks.

We played a round of miniature golf, went to the Butterfly Museum, which fascinated Wiley, and all but Sarah and Carlin went to another show. I don't remember who the performer was or why we decided to go to his show, but it was unforgettable. He played guitar and sang and pantomimed many Country Western performers. He was a comedian to boot. He had us laughing through our tears. His final number was breathtaking. He played Malaguena on the guitar using both hands to pick the strings. As a guitar player, I was in awe. I do simple strums and plunking. He was amazing.

The kids were tired of shows and when it was time to leave they were ready. Becky and I could have stayed another week. We cleaned up the condo, packed the van and headed home. We stopped to spend the night in Salina, Kansas. We got there late and had a bit of trouble finding a place to eat near the motel. We finally settled in for the night, with everyone anxious to get home now that we were headed that way.

We woke up the next morning to a Kansas snowstorm that had bound up traffic and turned the parking lot into an ice rink. Todd went out to help as many people as he could get their cars moving. Somehow we managed to get out of the motel and onto the highway with little trouble but a great deal of consternation about conditions that might lie ahead of us.

We drove about 20 miles down the road and the snow ended, the road was dry and it was clear sailing all the way home. It was a wonderful trip, and Becky felt so proud that it was her idea and she paid for it.

Someday maybe Becky and I can go back to Branson, just the two of us and take in as many shows as we want.

Just for the Fun of It

Joan is an incredible lady. I first met her when we were both in graduate school studying Recreation Therapy. I finished my degree, and she dropped out just short of writing her thesis. Within a year of two of graduation, the City of Boulder developed Expand, a recreation program for disabled people, with some urging from me and other parents of disabled children. I cajoled and carped and wheedled about the need for special recreation. I was more than the proverbial squeaky wheel, I squealed and skidded and slammed into the conscience of the recreation department. After months of discussion and data gathering they agreed to fund and develop a program for the disabled population in Boulder. It is still a most viable part of the City of Boulder's Recreation Program. It was cutting edge and a role model for special recreation in many areas. It's been in existence about 35 years.

Joan became the second director after its inception. She did a terrific job planning, organizing, facilitating and initiating activities that were appropriate and accessible for the disabled population. After several years she quit that job and set up her own program called "Just for the Fun of It."

"Just for the Fun of It" is a comprehensive and expansive program for disabled people. She sends out quarterly brochures listing the activities available through her company. Becky was fortunate enough to have the money available to take advantage of, not only the weekend programs, but also the cruises and the trips abroad.

Becky is one of Joan's favorite clients and her daughter Molly and husband Brett love Becky. She had all the attention she needed to be safe on these trips and have fun at the same time. Becky took two cruises to the Caribbean and two to Disneyland/Mexico. She has traveled to Disney World and Hawaii, Cheyenne Frontier Days and the

National Western Stock Show in Denver. She's in seventh heaven with all the animals in the Stock Show. I think if she'd been born without injury she might have become a veterinarian. She loves animals that much.

The monthly program includes Cinemax Theater, Boulder Dinner Theater, The Spaghetti Factory, pizza and movies, weekends at Peaceful Valley near Allenspark, Colorado, and taking the train to Glenwood Springs for a weekend in the Hot Springs. She is a well-traveled young lady who has the fortune to be able to participate just for the fun of it. Her brother has mentioned several times that he's never been on a cruise. He's happy for Becky.

She has been forced to take a hiatus from Joan's program for a year now. There's a very good possibility that she might be able to participate again soon. She thrives on social contacts. The phone and recreation are her outlets for social contact.

A note from her IP of March 29, 2011:

Strengths and Preferences: "Staff and Guardian report that Becky has maintained several friendships with peers for many years. Staff/guardian report that Becky is the "social glue" that keeps outings fun. Staff/guardian report that Becky is always up for fun and adventure. She actively participates in Just for the Fun of It vacations regularly. Becky currently has 3 vacations planned for this year, a Disney Cruise, a trip to a Dude Ranch and a trip to Glenwood Springs. Staff and Becky report that she participates in day trips with Just for the Fun of It at least twice a month. Becky's Person Centered Description states that Becky's peers report that they like Becky because she is so independent, yet almost always willing to access the community and spend time with her peers. Description also states that Becky has a great contagious laugh and that her peers also admire the fact that Becky advocates for herself much of the time"

That's Becky in a nutshell. She loves life.

Colorado Outdoor Education Center for the Handicapped (COECH)

In 1981 Ruth Wood School took a group of older students on an outing with the COECH. They were off to the mountains to participate in hiking and rock climbing. I knew people who worked there so trusted completely that Becky would be safe and secure. I was working at the time so I couldn't go along as a volunteer.

When I picked Becky up at school after her return from this adventure, the school's principal said to me, "I am sure glad you weren't up there with us, Holly. You'd have fainted dead away when Becky rappelled down a cliff."

How right he was. I am afraid of heights and would have looked the other way. The pictures showed her in harness with an aide rappelling down the cliff. Amazing!!

Bolder Boulder

When Becky was in her early thirties she called me in the spring and said, "Hey, Mom! I wanna do the Bolder Boulder."

I was speechless for a brief moment, and, realizing that she was completely serious, held my emotions in check and told her I would love to walk with her.

The Bolder Boulder is a 10K foot race that had its beginnings in 1979, and the 37th annual Bolder Boulder will be run Memorial Day, 2016. 2700 runners participated in the first race, and last year 54,000 participants ran through the streets of Boulder starting at the Bank of Boulder and winding through downtown to Folsom Field, the stadium at the University of Colorado. It has become the fourth largest foot race in America and attracts elite runners from many countries, mostly Africa and Mexico.

The elite runners start last so all the spectators in the stands can watch them finish. As the early participants finish the race they find seats in the stadium. By the time the elite racers cross the finish line the stadium is filled with fans. Music is blaring from the public address system; military hang gliders in apparatus resembling the American Flag float from above and land on target on the field; an announcer's booming voice keeps everyone informed of the status of the elite racers. It is a really big deal.

Becky and I prepared ourselves for the 6.2-mile walk; appropriate shoes, water bottles and layered clothes to deal with possible weather changes. The waves of the citizens' race are put into heats based on the participants' times in earlier races and their physical abilities. The letters of the alphabet designate the heats, the fastest runners being placed in the 'A' group and so on. Becky and I were back in UU or VV or somewhere near the end of the placements. It is a circus-like atmosphere with clowns and vendors circulating through the crowds of runners and spectators.

An air of excitement and anticipation permeated the whole area, which encompassed several blocks. It was finally our turn to start. Becky's gait is not conducive to fast walking; she still walks with a forward head and shoulders and is prone to get ahead of herself and lose her balance. My job was to keep her steady and walk a safe pace. Along the way homeowners had their hoses running to cool us off. Every few blocks volunteers offered water and Gatorade. Belly dancers entertained from another yard. The circus atmosphere continued throughout the whole route. Becky loved it. One year Brandon, her co-worker was on the sidelines in a gorilla mask cheering loudly for Becky!! She was elated.

We arrived at about the halfway point when Becky had to use the toilet. Now, when Becky needs to go, she NEEDS to go. A row of about twenty San-o-lets was up ahead, but the lines waiting for each of them were endless. I knew she could never hold out that long. In desperation I looked around and saw a family sitting on their porch observing the race. I pulled Becky out of the line of walkers and headed for the house.

"I am sorry to bother you,' I said. " This is my daughter, Becky, and she has to use the toilet really badly. She cannot wait in those long lines at the portable toilets. Do you suppose she could use your bathroom?"

"Of course," said a woman in a rocking chair getting up to show us the way. She most graciously allowed Becky to use her bathroom, and our thanks were profuse. I made a mental note of the address and sent a thank you note.

Becky at the Bolder Boulder finish line

We finished the race and were not the last ones to cross the finish line. It was a most memorable experience walking into Folsom Field with thousands in the stands cheering us on. We felt like we had really accomplished a great feat, which Becky certainly had. We found seats in the stands and waited to cheer on the rest of the competitors. We watched in amazement as the hang gliders landed on the big 'X's that were on the field. The atmosphere was contagious, and we were a real part of it. Becky had finished her first Bolder Boulder.

Becky and Bill with race numbers

She and I participated about seven more years before she decided she'd done enough of them. During those seven years she recruited some of her friends and housemates and soon there was an entire entourage of developmentally disabled adults walking in the Bolder Boulder. My sense is that she set the example and the others followed. Years after Becky no longer participated, the Boulder Daily Camera printed a story about that group of special participants. It has become a tradition within the Imagine clientele.

Dastardly DJ

One year when the larger group was walking, the DJ from a local radio station, who made a habit of giving each heat a title based on the letter of its division, was making his usual humorous, snide and sarcastic comments. He called the 'A' group the Aces, for example. When he got to the 'RR' division he said something like, "And here come the RR runners. Could that stand for 'Retarded Runners?'"

Upon hearing that, I stopped in my tracks. I literally shook my head as if I were clearing my ears. Did I really hear him say that? I had been a Bolder Boulder volunteer for the last few years and was working at the starting line. I excused myself and made a beeline for the radio booth, which was close by. On the way I nearly collided with one of the counselors who was overseeing the special walkers. She was headed in the same direction I was.

"Did you hear that?" I shouted.

"You bet I did and I'm going to give him a piece of my mind!"

We descended on him like a falcon after prey. I got right in his face and asked if he realized there was a group of young people with developmental disabilities walking in the race. He stuttered and stammered and tried to apologize, but I wasn't listening. The counselor took over where I left off. When I arrived home I called the station and registered a formal complaint. He was later fired and justly so, to my way of thinking.

Becky was a trendsetter. Walking in the Bolder Boulder was her idea. I wonder sometimes what she might have accomplished had she been born without incident or accident. She has so many strengths and is not afraid to try new things. She is adaptable and compatible. Aside from academics she can learn new skills. I feel sometimes that she could have been even more outstanding than she is. Of course, I am her mother, so what else would I think?

Weekends with Grandma and Mart

When my mother retired at age sixty-two she started a tradition of having Becky spend several weekends a year with her and Mart. Becky adored both of them. Mart had the patience of Job even though he wasn't her real grandpa. Mother always had a special place in her heart for Becky. It wasn't that Becky was her first grandchild; it went way beyond that.

Mother's only brother, Harry, who was born when mother was a junior in high school, was born with Down Syndrome. Mother was his self-appointed guardian until the day he died. I have tried often to figure out why she had such an attachment to Harry and Becky. My sense is their love for her was unconditional, something I don't think she experienced much in her life. They appreciated everything she did for them and with them and they did love her with all their hearts.

In the beginning Mother and Mart would drive to Boulder to pick Becky up and then drive her home at the end of the visit. Eventually we trained her to take the bus from Boulder to Denver. We bought her the appropriate bus pass and she figured out the rest once we'd made a test run. Grandma and Mart would meet her at the bus depot in Denver. It saved them time and gas money and put another notch in Becky's independence belt.

She looked forward to those weekends, never knowing what Grandma might have planned: museums, movies, the zoo? They were special times for all of them.

That all ended when Grandma and Mart had to move to assisted living. They could no longer have Becky spend time with them. Mart passed away in 2007 and Mother in 2009. I thought it would really be hard on her, but, as was her temperament, she adjusted and moved on.

Rafting on the Arkansas

Becky's brother-in-law, Nick, was a river raft guide. River rafting is addictive, and he went every weekend either on the Arkansas, the Green River, the Yampa or the Salmon. The whole family became addicted to river trips and talked about them all the time. There is nothing more exciting than riding the rapids and getting drenched in the process.

After Grandma and Mart took a trip down the Arkansas, Becky decided she wanted to go. We asked her over and over if she was sure. There was no doubt she was ready to take the risk and ride in a raft with all the rest of us. This is the lady that wouldn't go in the boat at Niagara Falls. We were amazed that she was so willing to go on the river.

The day came when we all met at the put-in and clambered into our assigned rafts. With life jackets buckled and lunch and first aid supplies packed, we headed downstream. The morning was beautiful, and the first part of the river was rather calm. She managed to survive the first few rapids with a happy smile on her face. Then the clouds began gathering.

The sky became darker and darker and gradually more threatening. Rain poured and didn't stop. We were all thoroughly drenched with no sign of relief overhead. For some reason Nick had planned a much longer trip than usual. When river rafting one is required to go to the assigned take-out where the vehicle is parked to take drivers back to the put-in. We had no choice but to keep moving downstream. Becky began to cry and soon was sobbing loudly. There was no consoling her. It was early evening by the time we reached our destination.

Ferrying the vehicles from one location to the other is extremely time-consuming, so once we reached the take-out we had to wait about an hour for all the cars to arrive. We had not planned on stormy weather, so no warm jackets or blankets were available. We were all freezing, but Becky was the most miserable of all of us. She vowed in a very loud voice that she would never go on another rafting trip. She was so brave to try and it's such a shame that it turned out so badly for her. We all should have realized that a full day was too much for her, even in the best conditions.

An Overnighter

Becky is very protective of her space and her belongings. In 2008 a dear friend was coming to Colorado to visit her sister. Her visit coincided with my travels to Boulder to see my kids, so I made arrangements to meet her for breakfast in Southeast Denver at 6:00 a.m. Since it was such an early hour I didn't want to disturb my son and his family, and I called Becky and asked if I could bring a sleeping bag and sleep at her apartment; we could have a 'sleepover.'

"Hey, Yeah!!" She said, "and I can sleep on the floor with ya."

"Sure," I replied. "It'll be like camping out!"

I appeared at her doorstep with sleeping bag and duffel in hand. We had dinner at a restaurant and then home to bed. At 8:00 we both crawled into our sleeping bags and about 9:00 Becky got up and went to her bedroom. I guess sleeping on the floor was not her 'bag'. I lay in my sleeping bag and read until I was drowsy, until about 10:00. I finally fell asleep and was sleeping soundly when the TV was turned on so loudly that I sat bolt upright. It took me a few seconds to orient myself. I looked around the room, and there sat Becky in her recliner, fully dressed with remote in hand, looking for the channel of her choice. I asked her what time it was. "4:30" was the reply.

"Do you always get up this early?" I asked.

"When I'm goin' to work," she answered.

"So, what time do you leave for work?" was my next question.

"At 5:30," she said.

"So, I guess I better think about getting out of here soon." I mentioned.

"Yeah!" was the only response.

I felt as welcome as a raccoon in a chicken coop.

I packed up my things and left with nary a goodbye from her. I drove to Denver and found myself in the parking lot of the Egg and I restaurant an hour ahead of schedule. Luckily I had my book to keep me company. When my friend Marilyn arrived we had a good laugh as I related the incident to her.

Wisdom Teeth

I guess I'm a slow learner. Becky had to have her wisdom teeth extracted. Her counselor, Zander, called me in August 2011 and said something enigmatic like, "Well, the dentist got as far as putting on the bib, packing her mouth with cotton and reclining the chair. When Becky saw the needle for the Novocain shot she sat up straight in the chair, pulled off the bib and said, "I'm not doin' this!!""

Not knowing what he was referring to, I simply asked him what he was talking about. It seemed Becky's wisdom teeth had become impacted and all four of them needed to be pulled.

I calmly explained to Zander that Becky would not be able to have them pulled in the dentist's office when she was wide awake and aware of all that was happening. She would have to go to the hospital and be put under anesthesia to have it done. Zander made all the arrangements and called me with the dates.

As Becky's mother, I felt I needed to be there for the surgery and for the aftercare to make sure she ate proper foods and that the healing was going as it should. There can be complications, especially with the lower extractions. A dry socket is no fun to deal with.

I called Becky and proposed that I would like to stay with her for a few days to cook for her and make sure all was going well following the removal of her teeth. I assured her that I would get an inflatable mattress, put it away every morning and not be in her way. Without hesitation she agreed, which surprised me.

I arrived the day before surgery and 'settled in' to what little space her apartment allowed. She was happy to see me. Glory be!! I had high hopes for the weekend. Her surgery was scheduled for Wednesday and I planned to stay until the following Monday.

The first day we went grocery shopping for soft foods: Jell-O, pudding, yogurt, ice cream, applesauce, oatmeal, eggs and the like. Since her stove had been turned off, I brought a hot plate and a couple of pans for cooking. I have always been one to plan ahead.

Zander was a caring, dedicated counselor who kept in close contact throughout this ordeal. When he found out I had paid for the groceries he thought it should have gone on Becky's credit card. I asked him how Becky shopped for groceries. It seems that each resident has a credit card for his/her use when shopping for necessities. He would take Becky to the store and turn her loose to do her own shopping. He would sit and wait until she had picked out all her groceries then double check that she had bought what she needed. He would then go through the checkout with her and pay with the credit card. He told me he never had to make any changes in her choices. She always bought appropriate items and enough of them. I was surprised again at her level of independence.

The surgery went well, though one tooth was much deeper than the dentist had thought, so she was in the OR longer than expected. I was just beginning to be concerned when they let me know she was in recovery. She came around very soon and I was given permission to take her home. We left with instructions for aftercare in hand.

Wednesday evening and Thursday went very well. Becky was very receptive toward my nursing her and preparing her meals. The hot plate worked like a charm and she had hot cereal and scrambled eggs and soup. We watched a lot of television and I read my book and knitted a bit. She is not the greatest conversationalist under normal circumstances. Add the pain of the extractions and the subsequent swelling of her mouth and conversation was nearly impossible.

I very calmly asked her if I could pick up some of the disposable items that were lying on the floor throughout the apartment and do some minor cleaning on Friday. She gave me permission.

The next day her sister called and while I was talking with her I walked into Becky's bedroom so I wouldn't disturb her TV viewing. I made the major mistake of picking up a few items that were lying on the bed within sight of Becky, and she became belligerent in milliseconds.

"Mom! Leave my stuff alone!" she bellowed.

I tried to cajole her and reminded her that she had given me permission the day before. She would have none of it. The expletives came out of her mouth like lava spewing out of a volcano. I was so taken aback that I didn't know what to say.

She was so ugly that I finally said, "Do you want me to leave? Shall I go stay with your brother?"

"YES!" was her firm reply, with a few added expletives.

In tears I called her brother and told him I was going to return home. He talked me into coming by his office before making any hasty decisions. I was glad I did. He calmed me down and made me see how silly it was for me to be tearful and upset about Becky's reaction. She had been quick to anger and foul-mouthed for a few years when bothered by friends and staff. She did not learn curse words at home; it must have been from her peers. She certainly knew how to use them. That was not the first time she had called me foul names, but it was the first time it affected me that way.

I called Zander and told him she was all his. It would be up to staff to make sure she was eating the right foods and cleaning her mouth as the doctor had ordered. He was more than willing to take on that responsibility.

In all honesty, I had a hard time even talking to Becky on the phone for a few weeks after that. My sense was she should have known better than to treat me that way. Who knows what goes on in her head? What she is feeling? What she is really thinking? She has difficulty expressing her feelings and when harassed the foul language comes out.

The Cleaning Fairies/A Ripoff

One good thing that came out of that ill-fated sleepover was discovering that the Cleaning Fairies, the house cleaning company that cleaned Becky's apartment twice a month, had not been doing the job for years.

Upon arrival that first day I asked to use the bathroom. I was appalled. There was toothpaste spittle all over the basin, the bathtub was anything but shiny clean, the windowsill had years' worth of dust and grit, cobwebs abounded in every corner of the room. The heating register was full of dirt and grime and the toilet was just plain yucky.

From there I wandered into the kitchen. The sink had gooey grime oozing out from under the edges; the top of the refrigerator was covered with a thick layer of dirt and dust; the floor under the refrigerator door had probably never been cleaned. It was disgusting. The most disgusting part of the whole scenario was that Becky paid $90 twice a month for two 'cleaning fairies' to come clean her apartment.

They were no dummies. They could tell that Becky wouldn't care nor would she notice. They did just enough to make it look like they'd been there. They vacuumed the living room carpet, which was covered with kitty litter and crumbs from Becky's meals. They must have swished around the toilet bowl and the basin, but no thorough cleaning could have taken place. The floor-to-ceiling louvered heat register in the living room was even dirtier than the small one in the bathroom. They obviously chose to ignore it. I wonder what they did with the extra time they had. They couldn't have spent more than half an hour in her space.

I called Imagine's on-sight supervisor, Michael, and let him know how upset I was with the whole scene. He called the Cleaning Fairies owner, Molly, who quickly called me. I hadn't touched a thing and would not until she came to see the job her employees had not done. Michael told me that he would always tell the cleaning ladies to call him when they had completed an apartment, but they never did. He apologized for not doing a better job of overseeing their work.

Molly came by first thing the next morning and was incredulous. She walked from room to room with me as I pointed out how filthy Becky's apartment was. She assured me that she would speak with the ladies who failed to do their job and would give Becky two months' service with no charge. I felt that it should have been a year.

After she left, I went to the store and bought cleaning supplies and rubber gloves. Becky had to be at the hospital later that morning, so any cleaning on my part had to be done the next day.

It all worked out well, because I could clean the kitchen and the bathroom while Becky was recuperating in her recliner watching television. She was not concerned about my cleaning those two rooms since none of her prized personal belongings were kept there.

I scrubbed and scraped and wiped and mopped and had things sparkling by the time I was finished. I called Molly and encouraged her to come and see what I had done. I let her know that it was a baseline for her girls to equate to. She assured me that they would do the work they were being paid to do. Michael also vowed to do a better job of supervising the cleaning of all the apartments at Timberridge.

The Cleaning Fairies had a long-term contract with Imagine, cleaning apartments when vacated along with apartments that were inhabited. I'm sure it was a lucrative contract and one they didn't want to lose.

The saddest thing to me was that anyone would take advantage of a disabled person the way the cleaning ladies took advantage of Becky. Unfortunately, it happens every day and in every venue. I am sure Becky has been shortchanged while shopping many times. She has no sense of proper change; she just likes to spend money.

The Walker

For the last few years her Labor Source counselor and Hoshi Motors had been expressing concern about Becky's balance and numerous falls. I tried to explain that balance problems were intrinsic to her brain injury and resulting disabilities. I felt that physical therapy would be a misuse of Medicaid because changing her gait was not going to happen. After walking a certain way for 45 years, there is little hope for making permanent changes.

However, the last couple of years I noticed that she hyperextended her left leg when walking and that her balance was worsening. She would visibly sight a spot, like a light post or parked car and head for it, holding on for support when she reached it. At the next scheduled IP I agreed with reluctance that maybe physical therapy would be beneficial for Becky.

She was scheduled to go to rehab at the hospital where I had worked as a recreation therapist. I called to request a physical therapist who I knew could relate to Becky. Jill was a character and knew how to make PT fun. As luck would have it, Becky had already been assigned to Jill. She was an outpatient for about a month, and the upshot was that Becky should have a walker. It would prevent falls, provide support, and help her stand up straight.

She took to the walker without any hesitation. It was like she'd always had one. Her supervisor at the Chophouse was most appreciative of Becky's walker. He said it slowed her down so she could walk with the group and it removed his fear of her falling. The Labor Source van did not have enough room for the walker in the vehicle, so picking Becky up would be a problem. I purchased a special attachment for the van which would accommodate the walker on the exterior thus allowing Becky to be transported with the rest of the 'crew'. The walker turned out to be one of the best things that happened to Becky.

Christmases

Christmas wasn't Christmas without Becky. When I still lived in Boulder I would take Becky Christmas shopping. Shopping with Becky made Christmas special for me; it was like the Christmas spirit had come early. We made a list and checked it off as each gift was chosen. She knew what she did and didn't want to give the recipients. It was either a loud 'YES' or a distinct indication that there was no interest in buying something.

It usually took about three hours to complete the list; a three hours well spent. We bought paper and ribbon and lots of Scotch tape and returned to her apartment. I would tag each present with the name of the person for whom it was purchased and then leave her to finish wrapping and tagging the presents.

She loved the job of wrapping the presents all by herself. She used yards and yards of Scotch tape, wrote out her own gift tags by copying the name on the gift, and then went about deciding how to get them delivered. Every year she bought a calendar for Joe, her 'boyfriend' who worked maintenance at the bus depot. He was an incredible man who took it upon himself to make sure Becky and her friends were safe while they mingled and waited for their respective buses every morning.

Every year she took a big tin of popcorn for her co-workers at Hoshi Motors. She delivered the family gifts at the annual Christmas Eve gathering at her father's home, and Wally and I were not a problem. She saw us often. Gifts for her friends were delivered to the bus depot where they all met in the morning. She looked forward to Christmas every year.

Wally and I moved to Montrose in June 2000. We had purchased an acre of land along the Uncompahgre River and had plans to build our home starting in July. The builder promised us it would be ready by Christmas. We moved in December 22nd.

Wally was working on the Front Range and brought Becky home with him that first Christmas in our new home. They arrived very late, and I had reason to worry, as it turned out. They had crossed Monarch Pass in a pounding blizzard. The snowfall was so constant and heavy that the windshield wipers couldn't handle the load. Wally had to stop several times to clean them by hand. At one of those stops, Becky decided to get out of the car. Wally yelled at her to get back in the car before another came along and hit her. He said he's never been so worried, and he is not one to worry. Thank goodness they got home safely.

Boxes and furniture filled every room. I had made sure the beds were put together and ready for sleep, but the house was anything but livable. Our Christmas tree was a small wooden cutout tree complete with lights I had purchased at a craft show earlier in the fall. Somehow I was able to cook a full turkey dinner in all that clutter. It was one of the best Christmases we've had. Wally took Becky back when he returned to work in the Denver area, without incident.

Travel by Amtrak

By Christmas 2001, Wally had retired, and Becky's travel to Montrose to share the holidays with us was in question. There was no way Christmas would be the same without her. I contacted her counselor, Elaine, who agreed to take her to the train station in Denver and put her on the Amtrak. She was also willing to pick her up on her return. It was all set, or so we thought.

About 11:30 that morning Elaine called to tell us Becky would be taking a bus that would not arrive in Grand Junction until eight or nine o'clock. It seems Elaine and her boyfriend had gotten Becky to the depot about 7:30 for a 9:30 departure. They checked her baggage and were guided to a room for people who needed help boarding the train. A bit later an Amtrak employee informed them that the train was late and wouldn't be leaving till 11:00.

Elaine, Becky and the boyfriend decided to go out for breakfast; what better way to kill time? They returned to the special boarding room about 10:00 and waited and waited and waited. Eventually someone came to take those in waiting to the train. One by one all the people in the room left to board and there sat Becky and her counselor. 11:00 came and went. 11:15 came and went. Finally at 11:30 Elaine went to see why Becky hadn't been taken. "Oh, that train left twenty minutes ago," she heard from the ticket window.

Tiny, but mighty, Elaine informed them that they WOULD get Becky to Grand Junction one way or another and they WOULD pay for it. After all, her parents would be waiting for her there. Amtrak called a taxi, got Becky to the bus depot and paid for a bus ticket for her.

We waited in Grand Junction and were informed that the bus was running late. Driving to the train station we asked if we could pick up Becky's luggage, which had come by train. The lady at the window informed me that without a luggage tag I could not take Becky's luggage. The train station was closing at 8:00.

We returned to the bus depot and tried to wait patiently for the bus. As 8:00 neared, I told Wally to wait there for Becky and I would go to the train station and try to convince the nice lady that it would be all right to give me Becky's luggage. I must have sounded desperate, because she did let me have Becky's bags. It would have meant another trip to Grand Junction the next day had she stood by her word.

By the time I returned to the bus depot, Becky's bus had arrived. Nine hours she sat on that bus without going to the bathroom. She got off so fast and didn't even take time to give Wally a hug. She headed straight for the ladies' room. I'm sure she didn't want to take a chance on being left behind when they made stops along the route, so she just held on. It was so good to see her after her long ordeal getting there. Needless to say, Amtrak would not be an option in the future. We drove her back to Boulder that year.

Todd and family spent Christmas with us a couple of years and graciously brought Becky with them. That would have been ideal for every year, but I encouraged them to start their own holiday traditions. It certainly was not their responsibility to make sure Becky got here.

Travel by Air

Well, Amtrak was out of the question. Finding someone who might be making a round trip from Denver to Montrose and back again was pie in the sky. Why not try flying?

I called her counselors and they were more than willing to get her to and from the airport. I was thrilled. I called and made reservations and looked forward to the day I could pick her up at the Montrose Airport, so much more convenient than driving to Grand Junction.

The flight over went without a hitch. She was excited because it only took an hour. Maybe this was the way to go for future Christmases.

We had our usual joyful Christmas with Becky handing out the presents and each of us taking turns opening them based on our ages. She loves opening presents, and, after the presents are opened, the dinner consumed and a good night's sleep, she is ready to go back home. I had learned over the years to make plans for her to be with us a few days before Christmas but to get her home as soon as possible after all the festivities. She loved being home in her apartment and in Boulder where everything is familiar. She'd have stayed longer if we had dog or a cat.

We took her to the airport, and, as seemed to be her luck, her flight was delayed for an hour and a half. We sat and waited and talked and watched people come and go. After what seemed like hours they called her flight to go through security. I helped her get in line and then went to get permission to go through with her. That took a few minutes. By the time I passed security they had her in a side area barefoot and spread-eagled as they used a wand up and down her body. She was sobbing! Tears and mucous were running down her face. I looked at the attendant and asked, "Why HER?'

"We only do the ones that headquarters tell us to do," was the answer. I was livid. Couldn't they tell by looking that she was harmless? I decided right then that United would hear from me.

I watched as we waited for her to board. The next person singled out for wanding was a gentleman who had to be at least 85 years old. He was fragile and shaky and another least likely to cause a problem. Following him was a family of five, a father, mother, two toddlers and a baby. I guess they can't be too careful! This was in the days before EVERYONE had to remove shoes and be wanded. I wonder how United made its selections of those to be searched. It didn't look like a random sample to me.

Becky flew a few more times without incident. The last time she flew was Christmas 2011. It was her first flight with the walker, so I was apprehensive. The plane landed and there she came down the ramp. Someone met her at the bottom of the ramp with her walker. She ambled over to the arrival gate without a stumble and was so happy to see us. A lovely young lady with blonde hair recognized that I must be Becky's mother and came over to greet me.

"Don't worry, Mother. I took good care of her. I'm an off-duty flight attendant and Becky just happened to be my seatmate. We had a great conversation on the way over. I am happy I was able to be there for her."

I thanked her profusely, asking her name. When I got home I wrote a letter of commendation to United Airlines for her care and concern for a total stranger.

Christmas 2012 found us driving to Boulder/Lafayette to spend Christmas with my children and their families. Becky was in the hospital recuperating from a serious leg fracture.

Christmas Blizzard 2006

On December 20, 2006 a powerful blizzard shut down the Front Range, the Eastern Plains and neighboring states to the East. All major highways out of Denver were closed. Trains and buses had been canceled, and thus flights out of Denver to Montrose could not be accessed. Becky was stuck on the other side of the mountains, and she so desperately wanted to come to our house for Christmas.

It was nearly impossible to explain to her that there was no road open for anyone to take her to the airport.

She would call me hourly and the call would end in tears. Her tears brought tears to my eyes. She was heartbroken. I thought and thought about ways to get her here, but none of them panned out. I was in constant communication with her counselors who were also brainstorming ideas to get Becky to Montrose.

On Christmas Eve I got a call from an Imagine employee. She and her boyfriend were going to Aspen for the holidays, and they'd be willing to take Becky as far as Glenwood Springs. The roads west from Denver to the mountains had been opened. Glory Hallelujah!! My brother lived in Glenwood Springs so what better meeting place than his house? I called him and he welcomed the idea of company.

Glenwood is about equidistant from Denver and Montrose, so we left home at the same time they left Boulder. Our timing was almost perfect. I think we were there a few minutes ahead of them. Becky was happy; I was happy; and the counselors were pleased that they could contribute to our happiness in such a profound way. Again that year Wally and I made the long trek to Boulder to take Becky home. It was the least we could do.

2012/A Year for Accidents
A Broken Toe

When I began to write Becky's story, it might have ended in 2010 with her working at Hoshi and The Outback Restaurant and living on her own with her cat Rocky at Timberridge. It would have been a success story, one that went beyond my fondest hopes for her. However, events occurred in her life in 2012 that caused major changes in her lifestyle in 2013 and beyond.

In July I received a call from Michael, the supervisor at Timberridge. I knew it couldn't be good news. He had not called me in the six years that Becky had lived there. Sure enough. He told me that Becky had taken a fall in the wee hours of the morning and 'stubbed' her toe. Jammed would have been a better term. It seems she had tripped returning to bed after using the toilet and slammed her foot into the foot of the bed. It isn't difficult to imagine her trying to catch herself and doing just that. The injury was severe and involved the bone of the great toe being forced back into her foot.

Apparently the skin broke in the process and blood was everywhere. She had enough sense of the seriousness of the situation to call the office for help. Her brother went by her apartment after she'd gone to the hospital and he said there was so much blood it looked like a war zone. She had tried to clean it up and stop the bleeding with paper towels. It must have been quite a scene.

An orthopedic surgeon was called in to put the toe back in place and suture the wound. It required putting in a plate to hold the toe in place. We thought for sure she would have to go to a nursing home for rehabilitation and would probably be confined to a wheelchair for a while. Surprisingly she was able to walk with a surgical boot and was released to her apartment.

Physical therapy was required before she was able to go back to work. She also had to be able to wear a regular shoe on that foot. Eight weeks after the accident she was released to return to her usual schedule of activity. Her counselors and employers were relieved that she had recovered so quickly, and I thought how lucky we were that it wasn't more serious. Little did I know what the future held.

Another Dilemma

Becky's brother and Sarah were to be married. The wedding would be held at the Boulder Mountain Lodge in Boulder Canyon. Wally and I had driven over for the occasion and were looking forward to being with family and friends. It would be a nice break from our routines at home.

We were so excited about Todd's wedding; couldn't wait to pick Becky up and head for the mountains. We arrived at her apartment about 11:30 a.m. and tucked her in the back seat with her walker, since it won't fit in the trunk. Her new gray slacks and mauve shirt looked great. She wore her new black 'Mary Jane' type canvas shoes with the Velcro closures and said she liked them. Actually, she looked really spiffy. She was as excited as we were about being part of this momentous occasion.

The wedding was a remarkable event with children and family running and laughing and crying and imbibing and waiting patiently for the food to be prepared by the restaurant Todd had chosen. Music was blaring from the sound system and a few people were dancing. Usually all that bustle eventually affects Becky negatively, especially noisy, boisterous children. She was content to sit and observe, laughing now and then at someone's antics. We knew she was enjoying herself, because she didn't ask to be taken home.

We left the celebration about 6:30 in the evening, as the sky was darkening. The deep walls of the canyon made nightfall appear early. The wedding revelers had built a campfire for added light Wally and I would have stayed longer, but Becky was ready to go home. We piled in the car and headed down the canyon, little realizing that plans were soon to change.

As we were walking toward Becky's apartment from the street, the weekend counselor, Dawa, intercepted us. He informed us that Becky could not stay in her apartment that night. We had no idea why.

He informed us that her toilet tank had shattered that morning, and the carpet was soaked. Professional carpet cleaners had been called and two large fans were placed in her bedroom to help dry the carpet out. The fans impeded her access to the bathroom completely, regardless of her need for a walker. It was like a major obstacle course. Dawa was concerned for her safety.

It was obvious she would have to go to the hotel with us.

She groused and grumped and plopped herself down in her recliner, announcing that she was **NOT** spending the night anywhere but in her apartment, and that was that? All three of us tried to reason with her, but her mind was not to be changed, or so she thought. Finally, in desperation, I suggested that she show me how she would maneuver the bumpy pathway to her bathroom. Dawa looked at me as if I'd lost my mind.

I walked beside her for security and watched as she gingerly stepped over the first fan using her dresser for support. The second fan completely filled the doorway to the bathroom. There was nowhere to step except over the fan. Becky accomplished that with some difficulty, using the doorframe for stability. She looked at us smugly, as if she had won the battle. Dawa let her know, in no uncertain terms, that he was concerned with her getting up from a deep sleep, being in the dark and somewhat disoriented in the middle of the night and trying to get to the bathroom safely. She stood her ground, frowning and muttering about not going anywhere else to spend the night.

Dawa gave me a look of desperation, and I finally had to use the only ruse I knew to get her out the door, in our car and on our way to the hotel. I reminded her that her birthday party was the following day and asked if she wanted it to happen. She said 'yes,' of course. I then took a deep breath and informed her that if she didn't get herself out of the chair, pack a few necessities in a plastic bag, and come with us quietly I would call all the guests and cancel the party. The final shot was to tell her that I wasn't sure when she would get her presents.

She was out of that chair in an instant and gathering her toothbrush, clean panties and socks and Blue Eyes, a Cabbage Patch doll that is her constant companion.

Once we arrived at the hotel and had a rollaway bed installed in our room, she was smiling and content. I really think she enjoyed watching Wally and I get ready for bed. She loved the hotel breakfast the next morning.

Unfortunately, after the birthday gathering, she was informed that she still couldn't spend the night in her own bed. The counselor's office is in another apartment across the street and up the block and has a bedroom and bath. She was going to have to spend the night there. They allowed her to spend the daylight hours in her apartment, requiring her to call the office if she needed to use the bathroom. One of the counselor's would then walk with her to the office to do so. She was much more acquiescent by that time. We left for Montrose soon after those arrangements were made, feeling secure in the knowledge that she would be well taken care of and safe.

She called Monday evening and said, "Guess what, Mom? Good News!! I get to sleep in my own bed tonight."

The carpet had dried sufficiently for the carpet company to lay new padding and replace the furniture. She was thrilled to be back to her regular routine. The new challenge was cleaning out her junk and rearranging her furniture according to the recommendations of an Occupational Therapist. Her safety is a priority. The counselors spent hours going through her mountains of clothing, both clean and soiled and her drawers full of junk. No clothing was found in any of three dressers, just papers and stuff she'd picked up in her travels through town.

Twelve loads of wash later, they still hadn't touched the closet. I informed her father and his lady friend that we needed to re-think gifts in the future. No more stuffed animals and Cabbage Patch dolls. No more underwear and socks until an inventory could be done on current supplies. I informed the counselors that their biggest challenge would be convincing her to keep her bedroom floor clear of clutter. The threat of having to move may be enough to assure her compliance, but only time will tell.

The most amazing thing about this whole event was that Becky had the presence of mind to shut the water off behind the toilet tank. It baffled everyone involved that she would know enough to do that. Her counselors were really impressed. She was always good in 'mergencies.'

The Straw That Broke the Camel's Back ummm Leg

Becky's being back at work and participating in extra-curricular activities again gave me a peace of mind that I hadn't had for a few months. I was able to go about my volunteer activities and daily routine without the constant fear that the phone would ring with more bad news. Becky called daily with her usual reports of work and play and dinner and Rocky. No reports of pain or frustration or boredom.

September, October and November passed without incident. December arrived and with it all the preparations for the Christmas holiday, baking cookies, making candies, buying gifts, knitting mittens and socks, decorating the house and planning for Becky's usual Christmas visit. Except for two Christmases, Becky had been with us to celebrate the holidays. I had made plane reservations for her round trip and everything was working out as planned, that is until the phone rang on December 6th. The caller ID told me it was Michael. My heart sank. He was the supervisor at Timberridge. It couldn't be good news.

And it wasn't.

I answered and Michael said, "Well, Becky's really done it this time. She fell stepping into her apartment and shattered her right fibula and tibia. She is in the emergency room right now waiting for an orthopedic specialist to do surgery."

No one knows how she tripped, not even Becky. When I later asked her what happened she told me, "I put my walker next to the doorway, put in my key and opened the door. Then I just stepped into my 'part-ment and fell."

"You didn't trip over something in the doorway, like your rug?" I asked. "Was Rocky trying to get out and you were trying to stop him?"

"No, there was nothing there. I just fell."

The tibia was broken in two places, shattered, in fact. The fibula had one clean break. The surgeon put a titanium rod in her leg because the tibia was beyond repair. An incision is made above the knee and the rod is threaded through the broken bone down to the ankle. The leg was not casted, so weight bearing was allowed. She stayed in the hospital for a couple of weeks and had intensive physical therapy.

She was discharged to the Boulder Manor's Rehab facility. Her room was filled with stuffed animals and toys, coloring books and crayons. When not in therapy or eating a meal, she was lying in bed watching television. That became a concern for us as the weeks passed, but she continued to make progress in spite of lounging in front of the TV during her breaks.

The staff loved her. The social worker told Becky, "If there were some way to keep you here, I would figure it out. We'd love to have you here all the time."

Becky has a great sense of humor and loves to tease. When her CNA would bring her meals she'd say in a loud voice, "Oh no! Here comes trouble!"

I'm sure she picked that up somewhere along the route of her life, and it was probably aimed at her. My guess is her co-workers at Hoshi Motors said that to her often. All her therapists developed a fondness for Becky. She tends to bring fun and laughter with her wherever she goes.

Her weekend physical therapist was a woman with whom I had worked at Mediplex Rehab in Thornton, Colorado, and she took a personal interest in Becky. Becky was in good hands. She had the gamut of therapies, physical, occupational and recreation. She soon became independent with toileting and could transfer independently into and out of her wheelchair. Our hopes brightened with the notion that just maybe she could go back to Timberridge.

Medicare/Medicaid, the source of her insurance, allowed six weeks of therapy and no more. As her deadline approached, it became clear that Imagine could not allow her to return to independent living. She had become too much of a liability. Their biggest concern was that the next fall could be even more serious. I believe they were more concerned about Becky's safety than any potential litigation. I had made it abundantly clear that suing was not my style. Still, the decision was made for her to go to a host home.

There had been talk of sending her to a group home in Longmont or Boulder, but the host home program seemed to suit her needs better than living in a group home with ten or twelve other people. She does like her privacy. The host home program involves living with a family who is willing to provide a safe living situation for a disabled person. The family assumes the position of counselor and caregiver. They provide supervision, meals, transportation, laundry, cleaning and medical supervision. The program has been in existence in Boulder County for about 25 years and has been most successful. Some host homes have had the same 'boarder' for that entire time. I reluctantly agreed to the idea in the interest of Becky's safety but was saddened at the thought of her losing her independence. So the search for a host home began.

The Host Home

Supported Living Services, the title of the department in charge of host homes at Imagine, determined that three homes might be appropriate for Becky. They set a date for her to go and check out their choices. The nursing home staff bundled her into the van and off she went.

The first home she visited was in Lafayette, Colorado, and belonged to Julie and Brian who had two kids and a dog. They had prior experience as host home caregivers and had remodeled their garage into a small private apartment with its own exterior entrance. I wish I could have been there when Becky visited them, because they wanted her from the first minute they met her and she didn't even want to visit the other two houses. It seemed like a perfect match.

Julie and Brian began cleaning out the apartment as soon as Becky and the counselors left; they wanted her to choose them and wanted to be ready if that should happen. Happen it did. It was unanimous with all concerned that this would be the optimum placement for Becky. They even agreed to let her bring Rocky with her, and she loves dogs.

Julie and Brian were host home caregivers for two other disabled adults. The first was a young lady who was not verbal and had some emotional problems. She had been one of Becky's roommates at the Manhattan apartments. I am not sure how long that relationship lasted.

The second was a young man named Randy who Brian met while working at one of Imagine's group homes. He really liked Randy and made the necessary arrangements for him to live with them. They finished the apartment for Randy's residence.

Randy hadn't been with them long when they lost their three-year-old son David. Julie had been visiting her mother in Louisville. Her mother's house backed up to Hayden Lake and her back yard was fenced and the gate kept locked. However, this particular day, someone had failed to lock the gate. Julie was saying her goodbyes and called for David. No answer. They called and called and searched the house. No David. Finally Julie looked out the back door and saw him floating in the lake.

The EMT's were able to revive him and he lived for about thirty days, thirty days that Julie and Brian were so grateful for. The brain damage was so severe that he didn't survive. Their grief was so overwhelming that they had difficulty dealing with Randy's emotional needs and outbursts. He had to move out.

Becky came along four years later. Their son Joey was 18 months old. Yes, they had another baby boy. Lily, his sister, was six. They were called by Imagine to see if they might consider becoming a host home again. They talked it over and decided to give it a try again. As already stated, they wanted Becky the minute they met her.

The Move

The apartment was spotless. They had moved Becky's furniture from her apartment and Brian had assembled it in her new living space. Her bed, her recliner, her TV and highboy all fit nicely in the space. The apartment included a small kitchen area with cupboards and a microwave oven. The bathroom was tiny with a compact shower, a basin and a toilet. The small shower was perfect for Becky, because it gave her walls to use for support. Brian eventually installed grab bars to make it even safer.

I had gone over to help with the move in some capacity. Becky moved on Thursday and spent her first night there. The room was full of plastic bags and boxes crammed with her belongings, clothing, toys and collectibles. Brian had made an effort to put some of her things away; clothing on the closet shelves, underwear and sox in drawers in the highboy, and some things hanging in the closet. A path had been made through the bags so that Becky could access the bathroom and the doorway to the main part of the house. It was not a very safe environment for her at that point.

I looked at the mountain of bags and cartons. I looked at Julie who was looking a little glassy-eyed and overwhelmed and asked, "Would it be helpful if I came by tomorrow and helped Becky unpack and sort through all this stuff?"

I had nothing else to do on that Friday and was more than happy to participate in this life-changing event. Julie looked at me and said, "Would you do that?" The relief in her voice and posture was palpable.

I arrived about 8:00 the next morning and confronted that stack of stuff. Becky was sitting in her recliner watching TV. I told her we had to get busy cleaning up her room so it would be livable. She turned off the television and we attacked the first bag. I gave her three categories and told her the only way it would work is if she cooperated and followed my guidelines. Of course, I put it in terms she could understand: one pile of things to keep; another pile of things to give away; and the last pile of things to THROW away. She seemed to comprehend the necessity to get rid of some of her things, and the process began.

I was amazed and surprised at how well she cooperated. We filled three giant trash bags with stuff to be thrown away. I never thought I'd see the day! Some of the trashed items were easy to dispose of. Her counselors had packed EVERYTHING in her apartment. I'm sure HIPPA had something to do with that. I'm here to tell you they packed the filthiest toilet brush I've ever seen and the toilet plunger. I wish I'd been the one packing her apartment. I would have cut the number of bags and boxes in half, at least.

She was willing to dispose of all her bus schedules, Boulder propaganda, fliers, brochures and other collectibles she had accumulated over the years. She was willing to part with some shoes, clothing, stuffed animals and toys. I hauled three large bags of donations to the local Salvation Army. Not only was she cooperative, she did it willingly and with a smile on her face.

It took us all day to complete the job, and when we were finished the room looked terrific. The closet was so organized and she could see all her clothing on the hangers. In her old apartment everything was so disorganized and cram-packed into whatever space was available that she wasn't aware of all that she had. Her counselors reported that they found bags of gifts she'd never even opened. The number of pairs of sox and underwear she had was incredible. I believed her when she'd call and tell me she needed sox and underwear and ply her with a new supply. She must have had hundreds of pairs of each. So much collected junk and refuse and poor cleaning habits hid the true availability of usable clothing. I put out an alert that no more sox and underwear were needed.

I do know that she never folded her clean laundry and put it in drawers. She had two baskets, one for clean clothes and one for soiled clothing. She dressed out of the basket of clean clothes. Of course, this explained why her tee shirts where always wrinkled and often threadbare. She wore them over and over again while new ones sat in gift bags buried in the closet.

Life in her New Home

Becky seemed to settle into the host home. She enjoyed the meals that Brian and Julie prepared for her and ate with the family in the kitchen. A physical therapist came three times a week to treat her and provide her with an exercise program. Julie and Brian were very attentive, monitoring her in the shower and making sure she took her meds.

In the beginning it was all new and exciting. The whole process was a learning experience for all involved. The kids loved Becky and Becky loved the kids. Becky went to church with the family and found so many people there who knew her, most of them through her father's business. The family was amazed. Brian said, "We can't take her anywhere that she doesn't know somebody."

They took her to a family birthday party at Dave and Buster's, a big venue for sports fans in Denver, and an old neighbor recognized her from their childhood days. It is true; Becky has friends everywhere. She rode the bus throughout Boulder for thirty or more years and made friends everywhere she went.

Another phenomenon that surprised her host family was how involved her family was in her life. Mom, Dad, stepdad, brother, sister-in-law, Dad's girlfriend all called and checked in with her or showed up at her first IP after discharge from the Boulder Manor. The woman who lived with them had no family support, and the young man's mother would just call when she was upset and wanted to 'cuss' them out. Our family was a breath of fresh air for them.

Not only were we involved with every aspect of her life, but also we were most appreciative of their willingness to take Becky in as one of their family members. I send them gift cards for their favorite restaurants periodically. Every family deserves a night out once in a while.

The family has since added another child to the ménage. Hazel was born November 20, 2013, two days after Joey's birthday and two weeks before the family moved to a new home in Firestone, Colorado. With the addition of Becky and Hazel, they outgrew their little home in Lafayette. They found a bigger home right down the street from Brian's brother.

Becky's room is now on the upper floor with steps to maneuver. It is reported that she does very well with the steps. Her legs are stronger and she is aware that she needs to slow down and watch where she's walking. In addition, she's lost about forty-five pounds since she moved in with the host family. They monitor her snacks and cook healthy meals. Instead of cokes and chips for snack they give her apples and bananas. She eats a lot more fresh fruits and vegetables and is no longer wearing extra-large sized clothing. Her balance has improved with the weight loss as has her self-esteem.

At last report her blood tests were so good that she has been taken off two diabetes meds completely and the other has been cut in half. It seems her weight loss has had a positive effect on more than her balance.

Julie has even convinced her to wear lacy tops and sometimes even a necklace. When I expressed surprise regarding her willingness to wear ladylike attire, Julie informed me that Becky is very proud of how she looks and beams when others compliment her on her appearance and weight loss. I just wonder what happened to my tomboy. I am thrilled, really.

Becky is left to her own devices now and then depending on what the family has to do. When Brian has to pick Lily up at school and Julie is at the doctor's with Joey and Hazel, Becky is on her own. The latest report is that she doesn't use the walker when she's in the house. There are enough things around for her to hold on to for her safety. Brian told me he worries about her falling when they're out walking somewhere, but that her lapses in balance happen more and more infrequently.

The only drawback to the move was that Rocky had to be taken to a shelter. He threw up every time he ate and continually missed hitting the cat box when he had to go. Someone said he was a 'scarf and barf' cat. He ate too much and then threw up. The vet checked him out thoroughly and they even tried buying him prescription cat food, but nothing changed his behavior. Julie didn't want him in the new house sullying the new carpet. Becky didn't seem upset that Rocky wasn't moving with her. She had not been paying much attention to him of late and, to boot, he had become an outside cat. He even spent the night outside and loved it. I guess after ten years of being confined inside a tiny apartment, the outdoors looked enormous. He welcomed it. We just hope they found a good home for him. He was a sweet kitty.

Joey and Lily call Julie's mom Nana and so does Becky. By all reports Nana loves that Becky calls her that. In the transition period Becky was dropped off at Nana's house after work and picked up there by Brian or Julie. They often have dinner at her house, and she watches the whole lot of them when Brian and Julie need a night away from kids and responsibilities. Becky loves her and loves spending time at her house. Plus, she has a dog. Whoopee!

Last Saturday Becky called later than usual and I asked why.

"I just got back," she said breathlessly.

"Where did you go?" I asked.

"We all went to the zoo and had lunch at McDonald's," she answered.

They watched the AFL Championship game together on Sunday. She is a huge Broncos fan. She'll call us after the game to talk about it, especially if the Broncos win. She used to bet a dime a game with my stepfather. She always took the Broncos and he, for the sake of betting, would take the other team. If she won, she demanded payment from him, but if he won he never saw a penny of his winnings. After he died no one was willing to take his place.

Becky is just part of their family. They take her with them to dinner, outings, weekends at the cabin, swimming, and shopping. They were amazed at how well she can swim. She surprises lots of people with her abilities. Sometimes Becky chooses to stay home for errands and short trips, but she's always up for the zoo and McDonald's.

I couldn't be happier with Becky's living situation. Julie told me once that Becky was 'cake.' She apparently is so easy for them to have around. She's pleasant most of the time and 'laid back,' according to Brian. Brian reports that she is even doing a good job of keeping her room clean and floor free of clutter. I guess she doesn't want another hospital stay followed by rehab.

They were warned about her temperamental outbursts and foul language during the planning process and did not seem concerned about that negative aspect of life with Becky. They have not seen any of that. When she goes to family gatherings everyone reports that she seems so happy and contented. Her sister exclaimed after one family gathering, "She's even groomed and has on clean clothes!" Maybe family life is what she needed.

I do know that if she were to live with us she would be bored to tears. We have no pets. We're old fuddy-duddies who are set in our ways. There are no programs in Montrose for her like the ones in Boulder County. She was invited to come live with us many times, but always said no. Besides, she listens better to people who are not family. Julie and Brian don't take any guff from her and they are very aware of manipulative behaviors, which Becky is capable of attempting. They stand their ground and she adheres to their rules. It is all so refreshing for me. We talk daily and she sounds so happy with everything going on in her life.

She is participating in 'Out and About," an activity program provided by Imagine, until they find work for her in Longmont. She tells me all about yoga and art and bowling, the National Western Stock Show, trips to Estes Park, and she hopes to resume participation in water aerobics one of these days. Her life is full. I am happy. I no longer ask the questions, 'Why her?' and 'What if....?' Becky has proven herself over and over again. As far as I am concerned she is unbroken, a whole person with so much to offer.

She keeps maturing and surprising me with new vocabulary and new ideas weekly. She is so capable. She has gone so far beyond what the prognosis was so many years ago. When one thinks of her beginnings, she is miles ahead of where anyone expected her to be. She's not through with this adventure called life yet.

"Hey Mom! Guess what? Did I tell ya? You're not gonna b'leve it!"

I can't wait to see what's waiting for her around the corner. I'll believe it when I see it. (1/31/2013)

Around the Corner (1/8/2016)

Observations

The birth of baby Hazel, added to the move to Firestone, changed lots of things. Brian had to work more, leaving Julie to handle the household alone. Becky was left home alone a lot more and omitted from some family activities without explanation. I didn't push the panic button, but began to get an inkling that things weren't as they should be. Something was amiss.

I asked Brian and Julie if they would consider having Becky's birthday celebration in their back yard. I would pay all the grocery expenses and bring the birthday cake, send out all the invitations and make all the other arrangements if they would do the grilling and provide the space. Brian jumped in with both feet. He loves to grill, he said. Julie insisted on making the birthday cake. It was all set.

Wally and I arrived for the party. The back yard looked great. They had a canopy and tables and chairs. All the invited guests were there. It looked idyllic from the outside.

Becky wanted me to see her room, so up the stairs we trudged. The family room was somewhat orderly as we walked through it, but the upstairs was in a state of total upheaval. Becky's room was the only clean room on the whole second floor. The carpet in all of the other bedrooms was not visible. The floors were covered with toys and clothes and shoes and stuff, a disaster waiting to happen. I admonished myself by telling myself that I shouldn't judge others by my standards.

I knew from the beginning that Julie was not the best housekeeper, but didn't want to obsess over that notion, having grown up with a mother who preferred clutter. I put it out of my mind and went back to the party and had a good time. How could I not? My kids and grandkids were there and it was all about family.

When I was back in Montrose I kept picturing the clutter and thinking what a safety hazard that was for Becky, especially if the downstairs were that disorganized. Still, I didn't think of doing anything drastic.

It had also become a trial for Julie to pick Becky up in Longmont after her program. Their home was in Weld County, just across he county line. The Longmont activities program allowed Becky to participate but could not provide transportation to or from the facility. Julie had to drop her off and pick her up. It seems the pickup time coincided with Hazel's and Joey's naps, so often Becky would sit for an hour waiting for a ride.

With some encouragement from me a program in Weld County was located which would provide a ride for Becky to and from the activities. Everyone seemed to be happy with that arrangement. One less thing for me to be concerned about.

Required paperwork & Revelations

Caregivers are responsible for filling out reports in a timely fashion, reports required by the government for various reasons. In November, 2014, Julie was remiss in submitting Becky's bank statements on time and Becky was in jeopardy of losing her SSI funding. Imagine had given her a deadline which she did not acknowledge, so they contacted me. I did not have access to Becky's bank statement but told them I would insist that Julie acquire it and get it in to the proper department before the deadline. With pressure from all sides, Julie gave the pin number to the financial supervisor at Imagine and the deadline was met, but just barely.

That pushed my big button. It takes a lot to make me react, but push my big button and it's all over. I called Becky's case manager Katie and told her I thought it was time to look for a new placement for Becky. Her reaction was one of relief. She told me that all the Imagine staff involved in Becky's case had been concerned for months about the appropriateness of her placement with Brian and Julie. They were so relieved to hear my request. It seems that getting required papers filed from Brian and Julie was like pulling teeth. They were always late and oftentimes not even submitted.

In addition, Brian and Julie had assured the staff that they would get Becky to and from her program, regardless of the fact that they now lived so much farther away. They had made promises that were not kept. I think they meant well, life just got in the way. The staff was very disappointed in their ignoring many of the requirements for hosting a client.

I asked why they hadn't said anything to me about their concerns. Katie's answer was, "Brian told us if we ever thought of removing Becky from his house, we needed to be aware that Holly really likes us. She told me if you ever threatened to find a new placement for Becky she would find another entity to oversee her residency with us."

That was a bald-faced lie and the final straw for me. No more questioning the validity of my concerns. When I enumerated my issues including the clutter in the house, I was told that, on regular visits by the staff, the whole house looked like a landfill. A path was made through the clutter for Becky to get to the kitchen. Safety issues? Health issues? I gave Katie permission to start the search process that afternoon.

By the next morning they had six houses for Becky to visit. I encouraged them to make her look at all six before she made her decision. Brian and Julie's house was the first and only house she checked out on the first go-round. It was obvious they were ready to get this done and with haste.

My letter to Brian and Julie came as a complete surprise to them. I iterated the reasons I felt their home no longer an appropriate placement for Becky and closed by saying I hoped they felt relieved and looked at this decision as a respite from too much responsibility. The third child put them over the top. They didn't need Becky's needs added to the mix.

Emily and Tyler

Becky chose a home with Emily and Tyler and Sammy the dog. The house is located in Broomfield, a mere mile from her Dad's house and much closer to her brother and his family. I think she fell in love with the dog, and Emily is a godsend.

Tyler, Emily's son, has a brain injury due to extrication of a brain tumor eight years ago. He is a delightful young man, soft-spoken, gentle and very bright. His limitation is memory loss. Emily has worked in the field of developmental disabilities for years and has a good handle on what is required to be a caregiver for Becky.

She blew me away at the IP conference where she was officially designated as Becky's caregiver. She offered to get Becky her own dog once Sammy died. Sammy was very old and expected to die soon. Was this woman for real?

When the subject of Joan Handley's 'Just for the Fun of It' was broached we were informed that Joan did not have enough room in her van for Becky's walker. Emily offered to contact Joan and discuss options. The outcome was Emily's willingness to follow Joan on outings in her own car with Becky in tow. Emily has since become a chaperone on some trips and is an erstwhile part of Joan's staff. This woman *is* for real and she's amazing.

Rules and Regulations

In Brian and Julie's care, Becky did nothing but sit in her room and watch TV and come down for meals once in a while. My sense is that Julie did everything for Becky because it was easier. When Becky first moved in with them she was much weaker and more unsteady. She required assistance going up and down stairs and supervision in the shower. Over time she became stronger, her endurance improved and she should have been more active in the household.

With Emily, Becky has responsibilities and consequences. They will not go anywhere on Saturdays until Becky has cleaned her room and done her laundry. Tyler and Becky do all the meal planning and grocery shopping on a weekly basis. Becky doesn't require a shopping list. She couldn't read it anyway. It's all in her head and she doesn't forget anything. Her memory has always been one of her greatest assets, and it amazes Emily.

Becky's bedroom at Emily's with her artwork

Becky goes to her program Monday through Thursday, comes home and joins Emily and Tyler in the livingroom. After dinner she showers and again spends time with the family before bedtime. They attend church on Sunday, shop for groceries and other necessities, and usually go out to lunch, one of Becky's favorite things to do.

Health Issues

When Becky moved into Emily's house in November, 2014, she was having horrific problems with loose bowels and incontinence. With Emily's diligence it was discovered that she had a major compaction in her bowels and a bladder infection as a result of not doing an adequate job of cleaning herself. After many tests and studies and a couple of hospital stays the compaction was finally resolved and a normal routine was established. Emily stated at one point that she hadn't "bargained for this", but she persevered and, though Becky still has accidents, they have worked out a cooperative system of handling them.

A colonography was performed during her stay in the hospital and revealed what the doctor perceived as a dermoid cyst on her ovary. The process began for scheduling surgery. Sometimes the wheels of medicine, aided by the government, turn very slowly. Finding an ob-gyn who accepted Medicaid/Medicare was a challenge. A doctor was finally contacted at La Clinica in Thornton, Colorado and the wheels were put in motion. Surgery was scheduled for November 24, 2015..

I planned to be there with Becky for the surgery and then bring her back to Montrose for Thanksgiving. You know the old saying, 'the best laid plans of mice and [wo]men etc.' My husband just had a knee replacement on November 10th and, after he fell on the knee while putzing around the wood stove, I realized he was not ready to be on his own. It broke my heart to call Emily and tell her I wouldn't be there. I was torn between two people I love very much. Not an easy decision for a wife and mother to make.

As it turned out she couldn't have come home with me anyway. The day of surgery the doctor called and informed me that the cyst was actually on the uterus, not the ovary, and he asked my permission to do a complete hysterectomy. I gave it to him most willingly.

The surgery went well; she was not discharged until 6:00 p.m. on Thanksgiving Day. Emily and Tyler sacrificed their holiday for Becky's well-being.

On the following Monday Becky participated in her activity program. No one could believe how quickly she recovered. She has a very strong constitution and a very high tolerance for pain. She was soon back into the swing of her daily schedule with no complications. Her last quarterly exam with the doctor resulted in a diagnosis of 'well adult'. We are hoping all that is behind us and she can truly settle into living a normal life with Emily and Tyler and Tippy, the new dog.

Christmas, 2015

Our neighbor, Fred, flies weekly for his job. He has more miles accumulated than anyone we know. In October he came over and asked if he could purchase airline tickets for Becky to fly to Montrose for Christmas. We were elated. He sat down at the computer and made the reservations in twenty minutes. When Becky was told of the plans she called everyone she knew and told them she was flying to Montrose to spend Christmas with Mom and Wally.

A dear friend, also named Holly, who worked with me in the recreation therapy department at Boulder Memorial Hospital and who now works for FEMA, has become one of Becky's buddies. When she is not on assignment she will take Becky out for the day. They go to the Denver Zoo, visit Holly's 'granddog,' have lunch out or go to a movie. Becky loves Holly and Holly has a great time with Becky.

On December 19th of this year Holly called and asked if Fred could possibly change Becky's airline reservations to a time that Holly could afford and, if so, she would be willing to fly with Becky and spend Christmas with us. Fred was an angel; accomplished that without batting an eye; and I had the peace of mind of knowing Becky would be well-attended on the short hop from Denver to Montrose.

We had a wonderful week with lots of conversation and laughter. It was so good to have a family Christmas again. Becky had not been here for Christmas for three years. It just wasn't Christmas without her presence.

I was amazed by her willingness to initiate conversation, her vocabulary and sentence structure, and her appropriate sociability. I feel, with the deepest confidence, that her living with Emily and Tyler and being part of their family has improved her communication skills to a great degree. When she lived in her own apartment, as great an accomplishment as that was, she came home from work and parked herself in front of the television. She had only the cat to talk to with an occasional check-in visit from a counselor. Spending time with her new 'family' is the best thing that could have happened for her.

Persons with developmental disabilities don't stop developing and growing. I think there is a general tendency among folks who do not have a personal involvement to think they reach a certain level of growth and then all progress stops and they're stuck at that stage for the rest of their lives. I'm here to tell you that is not so. She has even learned to use a cell phone.

For example, Holly took her out to lunch one day after their return to the Front Range and told me that Becky squeezed her arm and said, "I'm glad you went to Montrose with me."

A dear friend, whom Becky adores, lost his wife on November 10th. Becky called and told me she wanted to send Dick something for Christmas. No one told her to do that. She initiated it all by herself.

On Christmas Day Becky asked if she could call Emily to thank her for the gift. I handed her the phone and she made the call. During the conversation she said to Emily, "I can't wait to come home and see you and Tyler." My heart skipped a beat. She was happy living with Emily and Tyler!

I could feel guilty about my daughter not living with me. I could feel guilty that someone else is her caregiver. I do not feel guilty. My motivation for Becky moving out of our home in her twenties was twofold: (1) she desperately wanted to be on her own and (2) I wanted to assure that, if something happened to me, she would be taken care of by the state, and her siblings would not be obligated to take over her care. I didn't think it would be fair to them to expect that. I know they are appreciative of that fact.

Her brother is my co-guardian and has stated so many times, "I am here for my sister. Whatever she needs I will provide." He is such a devoted brother to her and would take her into his home in an instant, but with three young sons and a small house, it just wouldn't make sense.

Becky is in the best situation I could ask for. My guilt is assuaged by my realization that she listens to others much better than she does her 'Mom'. She loves me very much, but, after all, 'I'm not her mother anymore.' Ho, Ho, Ho.

Epilogue

Today Becky stands about six feet tall and weighs 160 pounds. She was petite until about age sixteen and then began to grow. She didn't stop growing until she went through puberty at age 18. It seemed as if all of a sudden she towered over me. I often wonder had she experienced puberty at age 14 might she have remained petite. My understanding is that growth stops soon after puberty is reached.

She continues to amaze me with her insight and her ability to adapt to whatever comes along. I spend minute amounts of time imagining who and how she might have been if her birth had not been so badly botched.

Would she have been athletic? I think so.

Would she have been attractive? I'm sure. (She is now.)

Would she have been intelligent? Of course! Our family leans toward the intelligent end of the spectrum.

What would have been her sexual orientation? Who knows? She is basically asexual and has been her whole life. Is that due to the oxygen deficit ??????

It is not worth the time it takes to ponder such questions. Becky is who she is and she is a wonderful, fun-loving woman who sees good in almost everything she encounters. Would that we could all be that way. Pimples, bad-hair days, or her status or lack of it doesn't depress her.

I once attended a seminar on Down Syndrome. The speaker was excellent, and during the question and answer period a member of the audience asked, "Do you think it is best to abort a fetus that has been diagnosed with Down's?"

The speaker looked at the questioner and said with such clarity, "Who's to say that people with Down Syndrome are not the leaders of the future?"

Total silence followed that answer as we all thought about the depth of the response. Who is to say what the future holds for people like Becky? She has certainly made her contributions to improving life and outlook for many people.

Of course, I would have preferred that she be born with no disabilities. However, since that is not the case, I cannot complain or feel sorry for her or myself. She is who she is and she is a pretty terrific person.

Copyright: January 9, 2015
Holly von Helms

About the Author

Holly von Helms was born in 1939 in Salt Lake City, Utah, and moved with her family from there to California, then Nevada and, at age four moved to Colorado springs. She graduated from high school in 1957 and matriculated at the University of Colorado in Boulder. She earned a B.S. degree in sociology and Spanish in 1961 and an M.S. degree in therapeutic recreation in 1979.

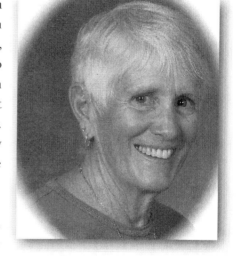

She is the mother of three children, Becky, Cindy and Todd. Becky, the eldest and the subject of this book, is developmentally disabled. Her disabilities are the result of injuries at birth. Cindy and Todd are the parents of Holly's six precious grandchildren.

Holly currently resides in Montrose, Colorado, where she and her husband Wally retired in 2001. Becky's story has been on her bucket list for several years. The fact that it is in print puts a big 'X' through that 'to-do' and is an accomplishment she hopes will make you laugh, and maybe cry and will be an inspiration to the reader, especially mothers of children with disabilities.